D0552213

I gasped at the illustration at the sta
out loud at the one at the start of ch
seldom happen. The start of chapter
I heartily commend this book which unashamedly speaks so
powerfully to the mind and heart of Jesus Christ.

Rico Tice
Christianity Explored

This book flows from the heart of a creative pastor/evangelist.
In *Why Jesus?* Geoff McIlrath engages with his readers in a
clear and down-to-earth way. He persuades us to take a fresh
look at why faith in Jesus is so important. This is a book you
will want to read and discuss with others.

Sid Garland
Africa Christian Textbooks

There has never been a time like this when Christians need
to be confident in what they believe and why they believe it.
This book points the way for any Christian to be able to give
a reason for the hope that is within them. Written with great
clarity, compassion and conviction.

Eddie Lyle
Open Doors UK & Ireland

This is my kind of book! I love the banter and the illustrations
are memorable but alongside this wonderfully light touch
there is real depth when it comes to examining the claims of
Christ and giving a very clear explanation of the Good News.
Why Jesus? is a great read and an ideal book to give to a friend
who is prepared to consider the message of Jesus Christ.

Graham Daniels
Christians in Sport

We have found *Why Jesus?* most useful in our prison ministry.
It is clear, convincing and very helpful to our inmates. We are
grateful for the availability of this resource.

Dorothy Boehm
Prison Chaplain, King County Jail, Seattle

I first read Geoff's book on a flight to London. On arrival I gave
it to a stranger urging them that reading it could change their
life. By the end of the week I was already planning orders of
the book for our evangelism training programme and café

church. Geoff has condensed the essentials into a brilliantly compact book that is easy to read and designed to change lives. I recommend you buy at least two copies, one to underline and keep for future reference and one to give away.

Mitch
Evangelist, Crown Jesus Ministries

Why Jesus? is a fantastic book for today's generation. It is clear, accessible and helpful to seeker and sceptic alike. This is an excellent resource for any church to use in its outreach ministry.

Sebastian Forjan
Church Planter, European Christian Mission, Slovenia

We have found *Why Jesus?* a great outreach tool for distribution at the Isle of Man TT races and other motorcycle events throughout the year. For people coming from different parts of the world with many questions about Jesus, this book guides the reader into a biblical understanding of why he came, what he accomplished and what he now offers to us.

Eddie Floyd
Fireblade Ministries

Geoff has given to us an excellent book that communicates in a very powerful way the relevance of Jesus to 21st century man. I gladly commend it and believe it is a very useful tool for evangelism in our needy world.

Val English
Pastor/Evangelist

In today's world the knowledge of Jesus Christ is greatly distorted but *Why Jesus?* addresses this in a very clear, precise, structured and easy to read manner. *Why Jesus?* presents the biblical Jesus this world needs to encounter.

Alan Dundas
Coaching4Christ

Why Jesus?

The continuing relevance of Jesus Christ in the 21st century

Geoff McIlrath

CHRISTIAN
FOCUS

Scripture quotations taken from the *The Holy Bible, New International Version®*, NIV® Copyright © 1973, 1978, 1984, 2011 by Biblica, Inc.™ Used by permission. All rights reserved worldwide.

Geoff McIlrath lives in Belfast with his wife and five sons. He studied Political Science at Queens University Belfast before entering employment in the banking sector. He has worked full-time with Castlereagh Fellowship since its establishment in 1993.

Copyright © Geoff McIlrath 2016

paperback ISBN 978-1-78191-767-1
epub ISBN 978-1-78191-797-8
mobi ISBN 978-1-78191-798-5

10 9 8 7 6 5 4 3 2 1

This edition first published in 2016
by
Christian Focus Publications Ltd.,
Geanies House, Fearn, Ross-shire,
IV20 1TW, Scotland, UK.
www.christianfocus.com

Cover design by Daniel Van Straaten

Printed and bound by
Bell & Bain, Glasgow

All rights reserved. No part of this publication may be reproduced, stored in a retrieval system, or transmitted, in any form, by any means, electronic, mechanical, photocopying, recording or otherwise without the prior permission of the publisher or a licence permitting restricted copying. In the U.K. such licences are issued by the Copyright Licensing Agency, Saffron House, 6–10 Kirby Street, London, EC1 8TS www.cla.co.uk.

Contents

Introduction

It's true to say that the name in the title of this book tends to provoke a reaction. I wonder what is going on inside your head right now as you decide whether or not to read this book. Perhaps you feel that you ought to read it out of a sense of obligation to the person who gave it to you. Or maybe you just don't get this whole 'Jesus thing' but you reckon a few minutes spent now will be worth it to confirm your suspicions and allow you to move on. It could be that you have a genuine sense of curiosity and think it's about time you knew where you stand on this issue. Then again, it might simply be that you are reading this because it was to hand and, as far as you're concerned, that's all there is to it!

What lies ahead if you do decide to read on?

As the title suggests, this is a book about Jesus. It invites you to consider what the Bible has to say about Him. It offers you some fundamental reasons why Jesus requires a response and should not be ignored. It seeks to explain why Christians think that it makes perfect sense to trust in Jesus Christ as Saviour and Lord.

So, it's your call.

Are you prepared to read on? Are you prepared to think?

Why Jesus?

Reason one

BECAUSE HE CAME AS PROMISED

Maybe you'll be asked this in a table quiz some day.

Q. Name the individual who has been credited with predicting the following:

- the Great Fire of London
- the French Revolution
- the rise of Napoleon
- the two World Wars of the twentieth century
- the career of Hitler
- the destruction of Hiroshima and Nagasaki by nuclear bombs
- the Apollo moon landings
- the Space Shuttle Challenger disaster
- the death of Princess Diana

How did you do?

The answer, of course, is Michel de Nostredame (known to us as *Nostradamus*).

It is probably true to say that if someone mentions 'prophecy' today, most people tend to think of the Bible (with all those funny sounding names like Ezekiel) *and/ or* Nostradamus. Perhaps he is the best known and most revered 'prophet' or 'seer' coming from the non-biblical world. Indeed, often people think that the biblical prophets and Nostradamus were really about the same thing. They could be placed in the one category because they possessed this common (and eerie!) ability to predict the future.

Is that a fair conclusion to reach?

Judge for yourself.

Nostradamus' prophecies come to us from sixteenth-century France. He began his career as an apothecary, working in the field of medicine and chemistry, but moved on to practise the 'dark arts' and was particularly interested in astrology. His most famous work is the rather non-cryptically titled *The Prophecies* which first appeared in 1555. Nostradamus wrote his prophecies in rhymed quatrains which were then grouped into sets of 100 called centuries.

Probably the best way to see how Nostradamus is used is to take a well-known example. What follows is, perhaps, the one most favoured by Nostradamus enthusiasts. To fully appreciate it, you will need to know a little bit of American history: namely that both President John F Kennedy and his brother (Robert Kennedy/Attorney General) were assassinated in the 1960s. Do note that the two prophecies come from unconnected centuries. With Nostradamus, you do not have to trouble yourself with context or an unfolding narrative!

> The ancient work will be accomplished, And from the roof evil will fall on the great man; They will accuse an innocent, being dead, of the deed; The guilty one is hidden in the misty copse.
>
> (Century 6 Quatrain 37)

> The great man will be struck down in the day by a thunder bolt, the evil deed predicted by the bearer of a petition; According to the prediction another falls at night, Conflict in Reims, London, and pestilence in Tuscany.
>
> (Century 1 Quatrain 27)

The Nostradamus faithful claim that what we have here are references to murder, the Book Depository, the shooting of Lee Harvey Oswald (who was innocent!), the Grassy Knoll, gunfire, Jean Dixon's warning, the fact that Robert Kennedy was shot at night, the student riots in France and England, and the Florence flood of the same year.

That certainly was enough to book Nostradamus a one-hour special on the Discovery Channel. Few would object to the statement that this is the best that non-biblical prophecy has to offer. This is their champion at the top of his game.

As we turn to consider just some of the many prophecies given in the Bible we will be better able to judge whether we are dealing with the same thing.

Look at me, everyone!

Jesus of Nazareth made a staggering claim. While discussing the Word of God with the religious leaders of the Jewish nation, He took their breath away with these words:

> These are the very Scriptures that testify about me … Moses … wrote about me.
>
> (John 5:39, 46)

Later He told His disciples:

> …everything must be fulfilled that has been written about
> me in the law of Moses, the Prophets and the Psalms.
>
> (Luke 24:44)

We need to understand what is being said here. In the clearest of language, Jesus of Nazareth is insisting that the entire Old Testament (as we call it) speaks about and points towards Him! He is its subject! Quite simply, if that is not true, then Jesus is the ultimate egomaniac and the greatest blasphemer of all time. There really is no in-between position possible with these statements.

It has been calculated that there are approximately 300 prophecies in the Old Testament concerning the Rescuer to come (the Messiah), whom Christians identify as Jesus of Nazareth. Sometimes that figure is further broken down and it is said that there are 61 major prophecies that chart the career of the coming deliverer. We will encounter some of these as we focus on the birth, betrayal and death of the Messiah. It is when we examine these 'word pictures' given in advance that we see how perfectly Jesus matches up against them. If you find a 100% correlation, it is impossible to avoid the conclusion that Jesus of Nazareth is, indeed, the promised Messiah.

Messiah's Birth

You certainly could not say that Jesus arrived on the scene unannounced. I'm not just referring to the star that guided the wise men or to the angels who frightened the shepherds that first Christmas. Actually, you can trace the promise of a coming Messiah all the way back from the manger at Bethlehem to the immediate aftermath of man's sin, as recorded in Genesis chapter three. God's promised deliverer would not just randomly appear. His lineage was mapped out for all to see.

He would be born:

- the seed of the woman (Gen. 3)
- the seed of Abraham (Gen. 12)
- in the line of Isaac (Gen. 21)
- in the line of Jacob (Gen. 35)
- from the tribe of Judah (Gen. 49)
- in the family line of Jesse (Isa. 11)
- of the 'house' of David (Jer. 23)

In a very real sense baby Jesus was the ultimate planned pregnancy. In fact, it was a pregnancy like no other. Christians frequently talk about the miraculous birth of Jesus. In one sense there was nothing special about how Mary delivered her child in that Bethlehem manger. But the process by which Mary *came to be* *'with child'* in the first place was utterly miraculous (read Luke 1:35). This, too, was something that was promised centuries beforehand:

> ... the Lord himself will give you a sign: the virgin will conceive and give birth to a son, and will call him Immanuel.
>
> (Isa. 7:14)

Because we are so familiar with the story of Messiah's birth, we could easily miss another significant detail.

Which parent of young children has not had the 'delight' of the school nativity play recreating the scene at Bethlehem? I write as a veteran of such campaigns, having had one child performing in the role of a donkey, and (brace yourself) another as the stable door! The only consolation is that critics labelled the latter a somewhat 'wooden' performance!

But why was it that Jesus was born in Bethlehem in the first place?

Caesar's first Christmas

Luke tells the story in chapter two of his Gospel. It really was the height of inconvenience. Mary, who was heavily pregnant, and her husband-to-be (Joseph), lived nowhere near Bethlehem. They lived in the far north of the land of Israel, in the town of Nazareth. But something happened over which they had no control. Caesar Augustus decided to take an empire-wide census. No doubt it was a device designed to ensure that everyone was paying taxes. Not only did he decide to take a census at this particular time, but he also determined *how* it should be carried out. Each male head of a household was to return to his own ancestral home to register.

Just think of the disruption for all those folk who had travelled and resettled elsewhere. But it spelled double trouble for Mary and Joseph. Not only did they have to set out on the approximate 80 mile trip from Nazareth to Bethlehem (allowing for a detour around Samaria), but they did it with Mary rapidly approaching her due date! If it had been left to them, you can be sure there would have been no travel plans for this couple.

But what Caesar wants, Caesar gets!

And we all know the story of the inn-keeper with no room, the offer of the stable, and the birth of baby Jesus in the humblest of circumstances.

So, it was all down to Caesar was it?

Not if you listen to Micah the Old Testament prophet. God had pin-pointed the very location of Messiah's birth centuries before it took place:

> But you, Bethlehem Ephrathah, though you are small among the clans of Judah, out of you will come for me one who will be ruler over Israel, whose origins are from of old, from ancient times. [or, from days of eternity]
>
> (Micah 5:2)

How amazing it is to see the sovereignty of God playing out in this situation. The most powerful man on the planet, for his own reasons, decides to conduct a census. He knows nothing of Micah's prophecy, yet his decision sets in motion events which fulfil the very detail of God's rescue plan for sinners.

I guess the real lesson is not so much 'what Caesar wants, Caesar gets.' It is, rather, that there is someone even greater than Caesar in control of history.

Messiah's Betrayal

Just about everyone knows what a person is getting at if they label someone a 'Judas'. The treachery of one of Jesus' own disciples, betraying Him for money, shocks and offends in equal measure. But we would come to the wrong conclusion if we pictured Jesus as some helpless victim outmanoeuvred by the actions of a traitor.

Jesus knew full well what was going on, even behind the scenes, as men plotted his execution. This was graphically illustrated when He shared a final meal with His disciples. Jesus told His disciples that He knew whom He had chosen and that this choice was made 'to fulfil the Scripture'. He then quoted a statement from King David in Psalm 41:9:

> ... He who shares my bread has turned against me.
> (John 13:18)

Within moments, Judas received from the hand of Jesus a piece of bread referred to as the *'sop'*. It was an expression of affection and friendship. Judas accepted the gift in his hand while simultaneously rejecting the giver in his heart. As the traitor departed into the night, Jesus told him to do quickly what he had determined to do.

No, Jesus was not a helpless victim. Again and again in the Old Testament, King David appears in the role of one who suffers for righteousness in his devotion to God. At times the description of his suffering far exceeds that which he personally experienced. As a prophet David was enabled to speak of the very sufferings of Messiah himself. Jesus knew that He was fulfilling in every detail all that was written, and that included being on the end of Judas' deceit.

But it doesn't stop there. The prophet Zechariah makes some stunning statements with regard to Messiah's betrayal. The context is significant. Zechariah had been instructed by God to act, on His behalf, as Israel's shepherd. The time came for Zechariah to ask the people to put a value on his work as shepherd:

> I (Zechariah) told them, 'If you think it best, give me my pay; but if not, keep it.' So they paid me thirty pieces of silver. And the LORD said to me, 'Throw it to the potter – the handsome price at which they valued me!' So I took the thirty pieces of silver and threw them … to the potter at the house of the LORD.
>
> (Zech. 11:12-13)

Don't miss the detail given in this rejection of Israel's shepherd:

- 30 pieces of silver are given (it is very possible that this was no arbitrary amount and was, in fact, a calculated insult. Exodus 21:32 states that 30 shekels of silver was the compensation to be paid if an Israelite's *slave* was killed in an accident)
- silver, not gold, is paid
- the potter is noted to be the recipient
- the money is brought to the house of the Lord (the temple)
- the money is thrown, not handed or laid down

Let's move forward through the centuries and come to the rejection of the One who presented Himself as *'the good shepherd who lays down his life for the sheep'* (John 10:11). Matthew records what happened and how widely known the unholy alliance between Judas and the religious rulers had become:

> Then one of the Twelve – the one called Judas Iscariot – went to the chief priests and asked, 'What are you willing to give me if I deliver him over to you?' So they counted out for him **thirty pieces of silver.**
>
> (Matt. 26:14-15)

> When Judas, who had betrayed him, saw that Jesus was condemned, he was seized with remorse and returned the **thirty pieces of silver** *to* the chief priests and the elders. 'I have sinned,' he said, 'for I have betrayed innocent blood.' 'What is that to us?' they replied. 'That's your responsibility.' So Judas threw the money into **the temple** and left. Then he went away and hanged himself. The chief priests picked up the coins and said, 'It is against the law to put this into the treasury, since it is blood money.' So they decided to use the money to buy **the potter's** field as a burial place for foreigners. That is why it has been called the Field of Blood to this day. Then what was spoken by Jeremiah the prophet was fulfilled: 'They took the thirty pieces of silver, the price set on him by the people of Israel, and they used them to buy the potter's field, as the Lord commanded me.'
>
> (Matt. 27:3-10)

There just was no denying the detail of what had happened in Jerusalem. That infamous piece of real estate nicknamed *'Field of Blood'* made sure of that!

Messiah's death

It is when we come to the events of Calvary that we see with unmistakable clarity how perfectly Jesus matches up against the biblical prophecies. The fact that Messiah would die and the circumstances of His death were spoken of in advance. That is why the apostle Paul could write that *'Christ died for our sins according to the Scriptures'* (1 Cor. 15:3). To feel something of the force of what Paul said, it is worth taking a Bible in your hand and working through the references below. Keep in mind that every reference from the Old Testament was written centuries before Jesus was born.

Forsaken by Disciples	Zechariah 13:7	Matthew 26:31-56
Silent before Accusers	Isaiah 53:7	Matthew 27:12-14 1 Peter 2:23
Wounded, bruised and spat upon	Isaiah 50:6; 53:5	Matthew 27:26-31
Hands and feet Pierced	Psalm 22:16	Luke 23:33
Mocked	Psalm 22:6-8	Matthew 27:39-44
Crucified with Criminals	Isaiah 53:12	Mark 15:27
Made intercession for his persecutors	Isaiah 53:12	Luke 23:34
Garments parted and lots cast	Psalm 22:18	John 19:23-24
Suffered thirst	Psalm 22:15 Psalm 69:21	John 19:28-29
His forsaken cry	Psalm 22:1	Matthew 27:46
Bones not broken	Exodus 12:46 Numbers 9:12	John 19:33, 36
Buried in a rich man's tomb	Isaiah 53:9	Matthew 27:57-60

Let's investigate further.

The Old Testament prophecies lay particular stress on the fact that Messiah would be *'pierced'*:

Dogs surround me, a pack of villains encircles me; they pierce my hands and my feet.

(Ps. 22:16)

… They will look on me, the one they have pierced …
(Zech 12:10)

… he was pierced for our transgressions …

(Isa. 53:5)

John's Gospel records three unsuccessful attempts by the Jewish authorities to put Jesus to death during His period of ministry. We are specifically told that they wanted to stone Him to death for the religious crime of blasphemy (see John 5:18; 8:59; 10:31). Some time later, when Herod, the puppet ruler appointed by the Romans, dabbled in a bit of Christian persecution, he had the apostle James put to death by the sword (Acts 12:2).

But Messiah's death would involve neither stones nor swords, but **nails**.

It was no quirk of history that, at this particular time, in the land of Palestine under Roman occupation, the state chose to execute a certain type of criminal in a specific way. The Romans would put to death non-Romans accused of sedition by the ancient Assyrian form of execution, known to us as crucifixion. And, as everyone knows, crucifixion necessarily involves the piercing of the hands and the feet.

One of the most unpleasant details of the crucifixion story is undoubtedly the heartless mockery of many who witnessed it. It is all the more disturbing when you consider that those conducting the cruel chorus were actually leading members of the religious establishment. Once again, it was written down beforehand. In Psalm 22, which Christians often refer to as 'the psalm of the cross', King David writes:

> But I am a worm and not a man, scorned by everyone, despised by the people. All who see me mock me; they hurl insults, shaking their heads. 'He trusts in the LORD,' they say, 'let the LORD rescue him. Let him deliver him, since he delights in him.'

> (Ps. 22:6-8)

Matthew records the taunts directed at Jesus:

> Those who passed by hurled insults at him, shaking their heads and saying, 'You who are going to destroy the temple and build it in three days, save yourself! Come down from the cross, if you are the Son of God!' In the same way the chief priests, the teachers of the law and the elders mocked him. 'He saved others,' they said, 'but he can't save himself! He's the king of Israel! Let him come down now from the cross, and we will believe in him. He trusts in God. Let God rescue him now if he wants him, for he said, "I am the Son of God."'

> (Matt. 27:39-43)

It would be a hard heart that is unmoved by that. Did you notice the detail given in both David's prophecy and Matthew's description concerning the passing spectators '***shaking their heads***'? It appears that the mockery of Jesus involved actions as well as words. It is a gruesome fact that with crucifixion the only part of the human body capable of any free movement is the head. Victims of crucifixion were known to writhe in agony for hours or even days in some cases. Could it be that, such was the callousness of those witnesses to the events of Calvary, they actually mimicked the distress of the Son of God?

A final one to consider

The apostle John describes the behaviour of the Roman soldiers responsible for carrying out the crucifixion of Jesus:

> When the soldiers crucified Jesus, they took his clothes, dividing them into four shares, one for each of them, with the undergarment remaining. This garment was seamless, woven in one piece from top to bottom. 'Let's not tear it,' they said to one another. 'Let's decide by lot who will get it'.
>
> (John 19:23-24)

Almost a millennium earlier King David wrote these words:

> They divide my clothes among them and cast lots for my garment.
>
> (Ps. 22:18)

As John remembered those Roman soldiers, who knew nothing of the Scriptures themselves but simply discharged their cruel duty (while seeking to have some fun in the process), he understood what was really going on. Therefore he continued to write:

> … This happened that the scripture might be fulfilled that said, 'They divided my clothes among them and cast lots for my garment.' So this is what the soldiers did.
>
> (John 19:24)

Objections

To my mind, one of the most compelling reasons for believing in Jesus Christ is found in His fulfilment of prophecy. In terms of both its sheer volume and the precise detail contained within it, Jesus of Nazareth is the perfect match every time. But not everyone sees it that way.

So, what objections are put forward? What alternative explanations are offered?

Can we be sure that these are genuine prophecies? Is it fact that these predictions really were made centuries before Jesus was born? Those are fair questions to ask; and easy to answer! It is actually a simple thing to show that every single Old Testament prophecy was around long before the birth of Jesus at Bethlehem. Around 250-150BC a group of Alexandrian Jews in Egypt produced a famous translation of the Hebrew Scriptures into the lingua franca of the day (known as the Greek Septuagint). All 39 books in our Old Testament were translated at that time. People may argue over just how many centuries back the prophecies go, but no-one suggests that they were written any time near the arrival of Jesus.

Okay, granted the prophecies were certainly around for a long time, but how do we know the New Testament writers didn't just make-up the different 'fulfilments' they describe?
Again, that is a very reasonable question to ask. Can you trust that what Matthew, Mark, Luke and John reported genuinely happened?

The first thing to note is that they certainly claimed to be describing actual history. It is worth quoting Dr. Luke's introduction to his Gospel in full:

Many have undertaken to draw up an account of the things that have been fulfilled among us, just as they were handed down to us by those who from the first were eye witnesses and servants of the word. With this in mind, since I myself have carefully investigated everything from the beginning, I too decided to write an orderly account for you, most excellent Theophilus, so that you may know the certainty of the things you have been taught.

(Luke 1:1-4)

It is the stated intention of the Gospel writers that their readers discover what Jesus actually did and said. Against that background, to accuse them of inventing stories so that they could present Jesus as someone other than who He was, raises another couple of major problems.

The authors were self-confessed Jesus followers. To practise deceit and falsehood to promote His cause was a non-starter. You don't serve someone who claimed to be *'the truth'* (John 14:6) by telling lies! And you have to ask yourself, why would they do it? When the Gospels were being written it was a decidedly dangerous time to be a Christian. Penning an accurate account of the life, death, and resurrection of Jesus was more likely to earn you a slot performing with the lions at the Colosseum rather than signing copies of your work at the Hilton!

No, the Gospel writers told it as it was. They were honest and accurate in what they wrote. Their task was not to make up what Jesus did but, simply, to write it down.

I might even be prepared to admit that Jesus does appear to 'fulfil' these prophecies again and again but, surely, someone was bound to sooner or later. A lot of people have lived and died. Could it not just be one incredible coincidence?
Does that have a hint of plausibility about it?

Not if you listen to experts in the field of probability theory. In case you think this all sounds divorced from the real world, keep in mind that the insurance premiums you pay are worked out according to statistical probability! A rather famous illustration of the probability of one man fulfilling only eight of the major messianic prophecies has come to us from Professor Peter Stoner.

He writes this in his book *Science Speaks* (pp. 106-107):

Coincidence is ruled out by the science of probability. We find that the chance that any man might have lived

23

down to the present time and fulfilled all eight prophecies is 1 to 10^{17} (10 to the power of 17)...In order to help us comprehend this staggering probability, suppose that we take 10^{17} silver dollars and lay them on the face of Texas. They will cover all of the state two feet deep. Now mark one of these silver dollars and stir the whole mass thoroughly, all over the state. Blindfold a man and tell him that he can travel as far as he wishes, but he must pick up one silver dollar and say that this is the right one. What chance would he have of getting the right one? Just the same chance that the prophets would have had of writing these eight prophecies and having them all come true in any one man, from their day to the present time, providing they wrote them according to their own wisdom.

I will spare you his further illustration, involving electrons, showing the probability of one individual fulfilling forty-eight prophecies. Suffice to say the number this time is 10^{157}. Yes, that is a number with 157 zeros in it!

Apparently you have a 1 in 14 million chance of winning the U.K. lottery each time you play. But in our case the odds are greater than you playing and winning the lottery *every* time you play, if you could play every week for the rest of your life, and then for many life-times after that!

Is it not the case that other people have made similar predictions that have come true?
There really is a one word response to that … WHO? History is littered with failed prophets and seers. If you found yourself somewhat impressed by Nostradamus and the 'Kennedy Prophecies' and think there might be some mileage in him, I have a challenge for you. Go read Nostradamus! Very quickly you will discover that, in addition to being translated in wildly differing ways, his prophecies are relentlessly obscure, vague

and enigmatic. With just a little imagination you can make a free-standing Nostradamus verse predict almost anything! But not even Nostradamus is to blame for all that he is credited with prophesying! Have you heard it said that Nostradamus predicted 9/11? Here's why:

> In the city of God there will be a great thunder, Two brothers torn apart by Chaos, while the fortress endures, The great leader will succumb, The third big war will begin when the big city is burning.

These words were read by millions over the internet in the months following the terrorist attack. The incredible irony is that they were posted by a student called Neil Marshall and used in his article *A critical analysis of Nostradamus*. Marshall composed the verse himself to illustrate how Nostradamus' style of writing is so vague that people will read into it whatever they want to see. That was one successful experiment! It really will not do to place the biblical prophets, with their prophecies of a coming Messiah, in the same category as anyone else. The prophecies of the Bible will withstand serious investigation. Why not put them to the test?

Christians are guilty of simply reading Jesus back into the text. You hang your 'fulfilment in Jesus' interpretations on the slenderest of hooks.
Really?

In Psalm 22 alone we encounter David speaking as the righteous sufferer who cries out to God in desolation, using the very words that Jesus quoted from the cross. He is scorned, despised and mocked with words and actions that are replayed at Calvary. He describes the agonies of thirst and having his hands and feet pierced. His garments are gambled for and distributed among those who afflict Him. Is this *'proof-texting'* or *'pre-figuring'*? What about Isaiah chapter 53? It is well worth a read:

> He was despised and rejected by mankind, a man of suffering, and familiar with pain. Like one from whom people hide their faces, he was despised, and we held him in low esteem. Surely he took up our pain and bore our suffering, yet we considered him punished by God, stricken by him, and afflicted. But he was pierced for our transgressions, he was crushed for our iniquities; the punishment that brought us peace was on him, and by his wounds we are healed. We all, like sheep, have gone astray, each of us has turned to our own way; and the LORD has laid on him the iniquity of us all. He was oppressed and afflicted, yet he did not open his mouth; he was led like a lamb to the slaughter, and as a sheep before its shearers is silent, so he did not open his mouth. By oppression and judgment he was taken away. Yet who of his generation protested? For he was cut off from the land of the living; for the transgression of my people he was punished. He was assigned a grave with the wicked, and with the rich in his death, though he had done no violence, nor was any deceit in his mouth. Yet it was the LORD's will to crush him and cause him to suffer, and though the LORD makes his life an offering for sin, he will see his offspring and prolong his days, and the will of the LORD will prosper in his hand. After he has suffered, he will see the light of life and be satisfied; by his knowledge my righteous servant will justify many, and he will bear their iniquities. Therefore I will give him a portion among the great, and he will divide the spoils with the strong, because he poured out his life unto death, and was numbered with the transgressors. For he bore the sin of many, and made intercession for the transgressors.

> (Isa. 53:3-12)

On several occasions I have talked with people who were shocked to discover that these verses were actually from the Old Testament and not one of the four Gospels. Perhaps they explain why Isaiah is often referred to as 'the fifth evangelist'. It is worth remembering that the early followers of Jesus were Jews who knew their Scriptures. It was through a fair reading of those Scriptures, and not fanciful reasoning, that they came to believe in Jesus the Messiah.

Could Jesus have manufactured this apparent 'fulfilment' of prophecy? Are you sure this was not all deliberately engineered? Could Jesus have 'customized' his life to make it align with the prophecies?
The first thing to note is that this view renders Jesus either a monster or a mad-man, or (perhaps) a bit of both! That's a difficult one to come to terms with. It means that the greatest teachings on morality that the world has ever heard and the greatest example of love that the world has ever witnessed, came from the mind of one who was a lunatic at best!

It really is a logical non-starter.

How do you engineer your lineage? How do you select your birthplace? How do you determine the price of your betrayal negotiated in secret? What influence can you have over what individuals decide to do with that money when you are nailed to a cross? How do you control what people say and do as they watch you die? How do you orchestrate events so that soldiers gamble for your possessions? How do you guarantee what happens to your body after death?

Surely it is obvious that, once again, the objections to the objection are simply overwhelming!

Moving forward
One fundamental reason the Bible gives for trusting in Jesus as Saviour and Lord is that *He came as promised*. He

possesses all the credentials of the promised Messiah, and the evidence is there for all to read. But this is only a first reason. There are others. As we turn to consider another reason, please note that they are cumulative. You cannot separate what you have thought about already from what follows.

Yes, Jesus came as promised, but there's more…

QUESTIONS FOR PERSONAL REFLECTION/GROUP DISCUSSION

1. Jesus claimed that the Old Testament 'spoke about and pointed toward Him' (pp. 11-12). How huge is that claim? Where does it leave Jesus if it is false?

2. Which, if any, of the prophecies in relation to Messiah's birth, betrayal and death particularly registered with you?

3. If you found any of the objections convincing, why was this?

4. Which objections, if any, have been missed?

5. Read again the passage from Isaiah 53 quoted on page 26. How many points of connection with Jesus can you identify?

6. What is your explanation for the 'match-up' between Jesus of Nazareth and the many prophecies of the Old Testament?

7. Has the material covered in the chapter changed your understanding of Jesus? If so, in what way?

BECAUSE HE REVEALS GOD PERFECTLY

Like father, like son ...

Before my wife and I had been married for eight years, much to our surprise (never mind the surprise of others), we had come into possession of five sons. As you can imagine, this particular arrangement has not been without its challenges. Not that long ago, for a memorable six-week period, we had five teenage boys at home together. As parents of that human subspecies 'teenager' (part adult, part child, part psychopath) will understand, at meal times the threat level fluctuated between severe and critical, and full riot gear was essential. Even an innocent request, such as 'pass the salt', could be interpreted as an act of aggression that led to an outbreak of hostilities. We could have exported testosterone on an industrial scale.

To be honest, it would not require any great detective skills to pinpoint the source of the problem. Our five sons share a common burden in life, each of them resembles their father to an undeniable degree. When old photos are produced, even after allowances have been made for the 1970s' haircut and accompanying fashion disasters, it is with an air of resignation that the boys will admit it's the same DNA at work in father and sons. But if the truth be told, this resemblance extends well beyond mere physical likeness.

Never was this more clearly demonstrated than in the twice yearly school visits for the boys' Parent/Teacher consultations. It was always a surreal experience to sit in my former school, listening to some of my former teachers, confronting in my offspring the very same challenges I had presented decades earlier. Admittedly the omens were not good. Hidden in my possession is the school report issued at the end of my first year in secondary education. Evidently there had been some form of staffroom collusion and it was payback time for the young McIlrath. All of my ten teachers, with one exception, restricted their comments to a single damning phrase, 'disruption in class'. And, lest you think that one kind-hearted teacher broke ranks to spare me the parental retribution that lay ahead, you would be mistaken. 'I think this low mark may have been deliberate', hardly helped extricate me from my predicament! Perhaps my old History teacher hit the nail on the head in summing up his cross-generational privilege of educating the McIlrath clan when he said; 'the apple never falls too far from the tree!'

Beyond resemblance

In this chapter we will consider the public ministry of Jesus of Nazareth as presented in the four Gospels. This covers the period of approximately three years during which the Son of God *'went around doing good'* (Acts 10:38) and that culminated in His death on the cross. What was it all about? What was going on as Jesus taught the crowds, performed miracles and touched the lives of many individuals?

The apostle John provides the answer in the final statement of his introduction to his Gospel:

> No one has ever seen God, but the one and only Son, who is himself God and is in the closest relationship with the Father, **has made him known**.
>
> (John 1:18)

John wants his readers to understand it was not until Jesus Christ came into the world that mankind could see the full picture of who God is. Not for a moment was John denying or devaluing the evidence that God had previously provided of His existence and character; the sheer wonder of creation, His interventions throughout history, His dealings with the nation of Israel and His word as recorded in the Old Testament Scriptures, all pointed men and women to the reality of God. But it was in and through the act of sending the Son that humanity witnessed God's climactic self-revelation as He fully and finally revealed himself in the person of Jesus Christ. When John writes that the unique Son of God has '*made him known*', he is saying that Jesus explains God to us. This is the centre and circumference of biblical Christianity. Jesus Christ does not merely resemble God in the way that my sons resemble me; Jesus *reveals* God, and He does so perfectly.

> The Son is the radiance of God's glory and the exact representation of his being …
>
> (Heb. 1:3)

> The Son is the image of the invisible God …
>
> (Col. 1:15)

> For in Christ all the fulness of the Deity [Godhead] lives in bodily form…
>
> (Col. 2:9)

31

That was what the public ministry of Jesus was all about. Jesus put on display, and offered for human inspection, the truth of who God is. He took people on a journey into the very heart of God. Indeed, so perfect was Jesus' revelation of God, He could say to one of His followers, '*Anyone who has seen me has seen the Father*' (John 14:9). To encounter Jesus, therefore, is to be brought up close and personal to God Himself. And this is why the written accounts of Jesus' public ministry are so crucial. Taken together, Matthew, Mark, Luke and John provide us with the God-given record of the words and works of Jesus in our world. The Gospels were written to help bring us to saving faith in the Son of God who came to reveal God and rescue sinners. What follows is merely a taster of the ministry of Jesus. The full accounts remain the most widely translated, printed, distributed and read 'books' in human history. Have you taken the time to read the world's best-seller?

Good to go!

The event which marked the beginning of Jesus' public ministry was His baptism by John the Baptist (Matt. 3:13-17). John was utterly bewildered by the turn of events that day at the River Jordan. Once more he had preached his message calling on sinners to repent, for the kingdom of heaven was at hand. All those who accepted they were not ready for the arrival of that kingdom made their way into the Jordan to be baptised as a visible demonstration of the reality of their repentance. But what confounded John on this particular occasion was that the King of this arriving heavenly kingdom presented *Himself* for baptism.

John protested. Of course he did! The one person in the riverside queue that day who didn't need to repent to be admitted to the kingdom of righteousness was its righteous King. But Jesus insisted and John complied. Only later, with the help of the Holy Spirit and the benefit of hindsight, did Jesus' followers understand what it meant. That symbolic identification with sinners in the Jordan at the beginning of His ministry served as a pointer to Jesus' actual identification with sinners on the cross, as the climax of His ministry. Jesus knew this was His divine mission, for He saw the heavens opened, the Spirit descending on Him like a dove, and heard the voice of His Father, '*You are my Son, whom I love; with you I am well pleased*' (Mark 1:11).

But there was a second inaugural event that raised the curtain on Jesus' ministry. Following the testimony from heaven came the temptation from hell. '*Then Jesus was led by the Spirit into the wilderness to be tempted by the devil.*' (Matt. 4:1). Finding Jesus hungry after fasting for a period of forty days and nights, Satan did all he could to destroy the faithful obedience of the Son of God, thereby disqualifying Him as the saviour of sinners. But Satan had more than met his match, for Jesus stood firm in the very situation, the wilderness, where the nation of Israel had previously, and so miserably, failed their test of loyalty to God. On each of three occasions the diabolical attempt to seduce the Son of God into compromise was met with Jesus' authoritative '*It is written …*'. The outcome of this opening exchange was Satan's retreat in defeat, while Jesus of Nazareth was declared 'fit for purpose'.

But what was that purpose? How did Jesus understand His own mission? What had the Son of God come to do?

Messiah's mandate
Luke records an incident that helps answer this for us.

> Jesus returned to Galilee in the power of the Spirit, and news about him spread through the whole countryside. He was teaching in their synagogues, and everyone praised him. He went to Nazareth, where he had been brought up, and on the Sabbath day he went into the

synagogue, as was his custom. He stood up to read, and the scroll of the prophet Isaiah was handed to him. Unrolling it, he found the place where it is written:

'The Spirit of the Lord is on me, because he has anointed me to proclaim good news to the poor. He has sent me to proclaim freedom for the prisoners and recovery of sight for the blind, to set the oppressed free, to proclaim the year of the Lord's favour.'

Then he rolled up the scroll, gave it back to the attendant and sat down. The eyes of everyone in the synagogue were fastened on him. He began by saying to them, 'Today this scripture is fulfilled in your hearing.'

(Luke 4:14-21)

Presumably the regular synagogue attenders suspected that this particular Saturday was going to be a bit special. Jesus of Nazareth was back in town, and had caused quite a stir in the days since His return to the region. But no-one present was prepared for what followed.

At a certain point in the service, Jesus stood up to read from the Scriptures. The scroll of the prophet Isaiah was handed to Him and Jesus, intentionally, located a specific passage (we refer to it as Isaiah 61:1-2 and 58:6, though our chapter divisions and verses were added much later). The first claim that Jesus made that day in Nazareth's synagogue is obvious enough, even if we are not familiar with the Old Testament. Jesus was claiming to be someone very special indeed. He was anointed by God's Spirit for a unique mission (the title 'Christ' means 'Anointed One'; it is not Jesus' family name!) He had been sent by the Lord to declare *'good news'* to the following classes of people: the poor, the imprisoned, the blind and the oppressed. We ought to think not only at a literal level but in moral and spiritual terms too. Jesus concluded His quotation from Isaiah by stating that it was His task *'to proclaim the year of the LORD's favour'*. Again, without any great knowledge of the Old Testament, we automatically understand that '*the year of the* LORD's *favour*' has to be a good thing. But it is when we appreciate the imagery both Isaiah and Jesus were drawing on that this announcement becomes something truly wonderful.

Year of Jubilee

Woven into Israel's God-given calendar was the Year of Jubilee. After a lapse of seven 'Sabbaths' of years (7x7=49 years), the fiftieth year was designated a Jubilee year. This was the best news imaginable for two groups of people: those in debt and those who had sold themselves into slavery. The Year of Jubilee meant the cancelling of all debts and freedom for all slaves. Jesus, again speaking in spiritual terms, tells His contemporaries He has come to announce God's time of Jubilee when He will cancel debts and free slaves. As soon as He spoke those words He stopped abruptly, returned the scroll, sat down and, with the eyes of everyone locked on to Him said, '*Today this scripture is fulfilled in your hearing.*' Wow! Jesus was informing the people around Him that, right there and then, they were living through the precise moment in history when what Isaiah wrote about centuries beforehand was actually coming to pass. It's as if Jesus was saying, 'All the waiting is over. I'm here. It's time to celebrate God's mercy and deliverance.'

All this is tremendous indeed but we have not yet entered into the enormity of what Jesus claimed was being fulfilled that day. And this is where we must check exactly what Jesus read from the prophet Isaiah. Let me quote you the full text that Jesus was working from:

> The Spirit of the Sovereign LORD is on me, because the LORD has anointed me to proclaim good news to the poor. He has sent me to bind up the broken-hearted, to

> proclaim freedom for the captives and release from dark-
> ness for the prisoners, to proclaim the year of the LORD's
> favour **and the day of vengeance of our God,** …
>
> (Isa. 61:1-2)

What Jesus *refused* to read in the synagogue was every
bit as important as what He chose to read. With absolute
precision, Jesus, as God's Anointed One, set out what He
had come to do and what He had *not* come to do. And
what Jesus taught on that occasion in Nazareth's synagogue permeates the entire New Testament. Perhaps the
best-known verse in the whole Bible is John 3:16: *'For God
so loved the world that he gave his one and only Son, that whoever believes in him shall not perish but have eternal life.'* That
tells us what God did, but the very next verse tells us
what God did not do:

> *For God did **not** send his Son into the world to condemn the
> world, but to save the world through him.*
>
> (John 3:17)

The amazing truth is that Jesus Christ entered our world
some 2,000 years ago to usher in the age of grace. God has
reached out to sinners in love and His righteous judgement is withheld by mercy. Or, to borrow Isaiah's terms,
the day of vengeance awaits.

But here we must be very careful, for Jesus is not saying that God's righteous and holy vengeance will never
come on a sinful world. Neither is He suggesting that He
will not be the one personally responsible for bringing
that judgement. But it will not come yet, and He will not
bring it yet, for He will save before He will judge. If we
fast forward to the final days of Jesus' public ministry, as
He prepares to go to the cross to purchase the salvation
He had announced, we hear Him speaking again of coming judgement:

Nation will rise against nation, and kingdom against kingdom. There will be great earthquakes, famines and pestilences in various places, and fearful events and great signs from heaven … For this is the time of punishment [**the days of vengeance,** literal translation] in fulfilment of all that has been written ... At that time they will see the Son of Man coming in a cloud with power and great glory.

(Luke 21:10-11, 22, 27)

The Old Testament has much to say about the promised Messiah who would *both* save His people and put down evil. Jesus' Scripture lesson in the Nazareth synagogue was His explanation of which part of God's programme He had come to fulfil. This is why Christians look back at Christ's 'first coming' some 2,000 years ago, and look forward to His 'second coming' at an undisclosed point in the future. Jesus of Nazareth will indeed deal with evil, but it is Messiah's mandate that mercy precedes judgement.

Look who's coming to dinner!

It would be almost impossible to read the accounts of Jesus' public ministry and fail to notice that on many occasions Jesus accepted the invitation to be someone's dinner guest. There was, of course, a practical reason for this. As Jesus explained to one would-be follower, *'Foxes have dens and birds of the air have nests, but the Son of Man has nowhere to lay his head'* (Luke 9:58). We should not lose sight of the fact that Jesus was an itinerant preacher, who was pleased to accept the offer of food and refreshment wherever it was extended to Him. There was, however, much more to this habit of eating with *anyone,* than the mere meeting of physical needs. And it was this very approach to eating that opened up a great fault line between Jesus and the religious rulers of the day. These shared meals did more than provide the locations in which Jesus taught, they were actually part of His message. To appreciate just how controversial Jesus' actions were in this respect, we need to acquaint ourselves with two very different groups of people.

Pharisees and Publicans

Even today the term 'Pharisee' remains in use, but it's certainly not a label anyone would thank you for pinning on them! This, however, was not the case when Jesus walked the streets of Palestine. The Pharisees were held in high regard by the people on account of their personal piety and deep reverence for the law of God. They formed a kind of holiness protest movement, and were famed for their strict discipline and obsessive obedience to the minutiae of their religious traditions. Experts in all matters relating to ceremonial purity, they rigidly applied a vast array of rules and requirements concerning the preparation of food, tithing and Sabbath observance. Such was their influence upon everyday life, they had secured official positions within the ruling Jewish Council (Sanhedrin) and had access to the Roman seat of power in Judea.

But Jesus' appraisal of the Pharisees could not be further removed from both their self-assessment and public perception. Like John the Baptist before Him, Jesus labelled them a *'brood of vipers'* (Matt. 3:7; 23:33). Chapter 23 of Matthew's Gospel makes for uncomfortable reading, for it contains the most withering denunciation that ever came from the mouth of Jesus. The Pharisees were *'hypocrites'*, concentrating on externals and consumed by details, while ignoring the important matters of justice, mercy and faithfulness. They were *'blind guides'* for the people who looked to them for spiritual direction, not just utterly useless, but positively dangerous. They weighed people down by placing upon them burdensome rules that they could never hope to keep. They were *'whitewashed tombs'*, impressive on the outside but on the inside full of death and decay. In summary, the Pharisees were men *'who were confident of their own righteousness and looked down on everybody else ...'* (Luke 18:9).

Firmly fixed at the opposite end of the righteousness spectrum were the publicans. The Pharisees enjoyed the respect of the people and expected to pass when examined by the law of God. But the publicans endured the contempt of their fellow citizens and knew they were in trouble before such a holy God.

The term 'publican', popular in older translations, requires some explanation. The Roman tribute was collected throughout the empire by the 'publicani'. We should not think in terms of how we view Revenue & Customs officials today: whilst government tax collectors may not bathe in public affection, their first century Judean counterparts were objects of real contempt. For starters, tax collectors were collaborators. They acted as agents of the occupying power. From their fellow countrymen they extracted a succession of tithes, tributes, taxes and tolls that ended up in the Roman exchequer. But the reason for their unpopularity didn't stop there. Every tax gathered would be sure to include a healthy surcharge to be pocketed by the collector himself. The community as a whole, and the religious leaders in particular, left the tax collectors in no doubt where they stood. They were banned from the synagogue and viewed as ceremonially unclean on account of their association with Gentiles and their choice to work on the Sabbath. Crucially, the people were instructed by their leaders not to eat with such 'sinners'.

The gathering storm

The following extracts from Luke's Gospel flag up the collision that lay ahead:

… one of the Pharisees invited Jesus to have dinner with him, he went to the Pharisee's house and reclined at the table.

(7:36)

When Jesus had finished speaking, a Pharisee invited him to eat with him; so he went in and reclined at the table.

(11:37)

One Sabbath, when Jesus went to eat in the house of a prominent Pharisee …

(14:1)

No controversial headlines there: 'Jesus dines with respectable society!' But, now try this.

… Jesus went out and saw a tax collector by the name of Levi sitting at his tax booth. 'Follow me,' Jesus said to him, and Levi got up, left everything and followed him. Then Levi held a great banquet for Jesus at his house, and a large crowd of tax collectors and others were eating with them.

(5:27-29)

Or how about this, when Jesus entered Jericho and encountered its notorious chief of tax.

A man was there by the name of Zacchaeus; he was a chief tax collector and was wealthy. He wanted to see who Jesus was, but because he was short he could not see over the crowd. So he ran ahead and climbed a sycamore-fig tree to see him, since Jesus was coming that way.

When Jesus reached the spot, he looked up and said to him, 'Zacchaeus, come down immediately. I must stay at your house today.' So he came down at once and welcomed him gladly.

All the people saw this and began to mutter, 'He has gone to be the guest of a sinner.'

(19:2-7)

This was going to lead to trouble. The three meals in the homes of the Pharisees had not gone at all well. Jesus rebuked His first host for his sense of superiority and the total absence of the common conventions of hospitality towards Him. To make matters worse, He commended a gate-crashing prostitute for her reverent affection and assured her of the forgiveness of all her sin (Luke 7:36-50 really is astonishing reading). His second host suffered from holy obsessive compulsive disorder, and was a fanatic on the issue of hand washing. The third was on high alert because Jesus dared heal a man on the Sabbath. Jesus was fully aware of the smear campaign that was underway against Him: *'Here is a glutton and a drunkard, a friend of tax collectors and sinners'* (Luke 7:34).

What a contrast in the homes of the despised tax collectors for *'...even the tax collectors, when they heard Jesus' words, acknowledged that God's way was right ...'* (Luke 7:29), *' ...there were many who followed him'* (Mark 2:15). In fact, they trusted in Him in such numbers that Jesus could say to the leaders of the religious establishment, *'Truly I tell you, the tax collectors and the prostitutes are entering the kingdom of God ahead of you'* (Matt. 21:31).

All of this begs the question, 'Why?' Why did these religious and respected Pharisees reject Jesus, while the shunned and sinful publicans received Him? Jesus Himself answered that when He felt the disapproval of the Pharisees bearing down upon Him:

> It is not the healthy who need a doctor, but those who are ill. I have not come to call the righteous, but sinners to repentance.
>
> (Luke 5:31-32)

How we all need to learn the lesson of the Pharisees and the publicans. If we cling to our self-righteousness, and thus refuse to acknowledge our need of forgiveness, we exclude ourselves from all that Christ came to secure on behalf of **sinners**.

> To some who were confident of their own righteous-ness and looked down on everyone else, Jesus told this parable: 'Two men went up to the temple to pray, one a Pharisee and the other a tax collector. The Pharisee stood by himself and prayed: "God, I thank you that I am not like other people – robbers, evildoers, adulterers – or even like this tax collector. I fast twice a week and give a tenth of all I get."
>
> 'But the tax collector stood at a distance. He would not even look up to heaven, but beat his breast and said, "God, have mercy on me, a sinner."
>
> 'I tell you that this man, rather than the other, went home justified before God. For all those who exalt them-selves will be humbled, and those who humble them-selves will be exalted.'
>
> (Luke 18:9-14)

Messiah's miracles

The apostle Peter stood to his feet to address the Jerusa-lem crowds who some weeks earlier had cheered for the crucifixion of Jesus:

> Fellow Israelites, listen to this: Jesus of Nazareth was a man accredited by God to you by miracles, wonders and signs, which God did among you through him, as you yourselves know.
>
> (Acts 2:22)

The accusation Peter was levelling at his hearers was that God had supplied them with abundant and incontest-able evidence that Jesus of Nazareth was, indeed, their promised Messiah. And the currency in which that con-firmation came was the mighty works He performed. But evidence that was obvious and undeniable to the people then, plays out very differently with modern men and women. There is no shortage of voices today that deny the possibility or, at the very least, doubt the credibility of the miracles of Jesus.

First, consider the objection of those who insist that miracles, including those claimed for Jesus in the four Gospels, are impossible. This view rests completely on a prior commitment to materialism and its underlying assumption of a self-generating universe. If, however, our cosmos is the result of the creative will and activity of an unimaginably powerful and intelligent being who called it into existence, then miracles, as His interventions in our world, are entirely possible. Even die-hard opponents of Christianity will acknowledge that it cannot be proved that miracles are impossible, for it cannot be proved that God does not exist. If you concede the possibility of God, the possibility of miracles is a logical consequence.

Being open to the possibility of miracles at the philosophical level is one thing, but can we be confident that the accounts of the miracles of Jesus, as contained in the Gospels, are historically reliable? Can you trust the stories they tell of the hungry being fed, the sick cured and the dead raised?

Of all that could be said in response, consider this. There was one group of people, more than any other, who would have dearly loved to have disproved the reality of Jesus' miracles: the Jewish religious rulers. No group scrutinized Him more closely, and none were more driven by the desire to discredit Jesus as an imposter, than these men. Who better to expose the whole charade and clear up the fact that the 'miracles' never happened in the first place? What we find, however, is the unwavering official line that Jesus performed all His miracles as an agent of Satan (e.g. Matt. 12:24). Never on one occasion did the religious authorities deny the reality of Jesus' miracles; instead all of their efforts were focussed on disputing the

43

source of His very obvious power. How simple it would all have been for the hostile authorities if no miracles had occurred. They didn't have that luxury, however, for the miracles of Jesus were undeniable events.

So, what are we to make of Jesus' miracles?

Who is this?

Perhaps the first thing to note is that Jesus' miracles, in a very obvious way, revealed His **compassion** for struggling, suffering people. Indeed, the oft-repeated phrase that Jesus was 'moved with compassion' provides the context for many of the miracle accounts. Even a young child will understand the most elementary lesson of the miracles; the Son of God was not indifferent to the burdens of those around Him. Jesus cared for the diseased, the disabled, the bereaved and the oppressed and He reached forth a healing hand or spoke an authoritative word to release and to restore.

But, the miracles did more than disclose Jesus' heart of compassion, they provided unmistakable evidence of His true **identity**. Who but God could rebuke the wind and the waves and command calm in their place? (Matt. 8:26). Who but God could take a young boy's lunch, multiply it in His hands and feed a crowd of thousands? (Matt. 14:19). Who but God could speak into a rock tomb and summon a corpse back to life? (John 11:43). From their privileged vantage point, the disciples asked the obvious question we would do well to ask ourselves, *'What kind of man is this?'* (Matt. 8:27).

Furthermore, Jesus' miracles were demonstrations of His **authority**. No-one or nothing was able to resist His power. All creation must bow before its maker, and that included even the rebellious realm of Satan. It was said of the notorious demoniac of the Gerasenes, who lived among the tombs and snapped his chains, that no man could tame him. Yet Jesus could speak the word, and leave him dressed and in his right mind (Mark 5:15). Satan's strongholds were no more off-limits to Christ than anywhere else. Even death itself could not have the last word if Jesus spoke against it. A father received back his little daughter (Mark 5:23), a widow her only son (Luke 7:12) and two sisters their beloved brother (John 11:2).

It was Jesus Himself who taught that His miracles were concrete evidence that the kingdom of God had come, '... *if I drive out demons by the finger of God, then the kingdom of God has come to you'* (Luke 11:20). The heavenly king had come, and His merciful acts of power provided men with His **royal credentials**. What a glimpse those miracles give us of that glorious kingdom which will come in all its fulness when Jesus returns and is acknowledged as King of kings and Lord of lords (Rev. 19:16). Christ's eternal kingdom is one in which sin, death and hell have no part to play. The miracles are foretastes of the perfection to come, tokens of that wholeness and restoration, and down-payments of all that awaits the subjects of His realm.

He who has ears to hear ...
Before leaving the miracles of Jesus, let's take time to consider one that is often overlooked. It is Jesus' final miracle, occurring in the highly charged circumstances surrounding His arrest, when Jesus and His disciples are in the Garden of Gethsemane on the night before His crucifixion.

> While he was still speaking a crowd came up, and the man who was called Judas, one of the Twelve, was leading them. He approached Jesus to kiss him, but Jesus asked him, 'Judas, are you betraying the Son of Man with a kiss?' When Jesus' followers saw what was going to happen, they said, 'Lord, should we strike with our swords?' And one of them struck the servant of the high priest, cutting

45

off his right ear. But Jesus answered, 'No more of this!' And he touched the man's ear and healed him.

(Luke 22:47-51)

The scene is one of unbearable tension. A mob has descended upon the secluded place to which Jesus had withdrawn to pray in preparation for all He knew lay ahead of Him. Following positive identification, through the greeting-kiss of the betrayer, the servant of the high priest wasted no time in stepping forward to seize Jesus. The disciples were at breaking point. Is this it? Is this the 'do or die' moment when they must take their stand and do their bit to establish the kingdom of God on earth? Surely if they start, Messiah will summon the armies of heaven and destroy their enemies! One of them decides to go for it, lashing out with his sword, and lopping off the ear of the arresting official. John identifies the individuals concerned as Peter and Malchus (John 18:10). Peter had not been attempting ear surgery! He took the head shot as he led the charge. But therein lay the problem. What charge? Jesus immediately put a stop to the skirmish and commanded Peter to put his sword away. Did Peter not realise that, right there and then, Jesus could have called down more than twelve legions of angels if He so wished? Incidentally, a Roman legion consisted of 6,000 men, so that's a minimum of 72,000 angels, each presumably with access to a heavenly arsenal! But, Jesus continued, '...how then would the Scriptures be fulfilled that say it must happen in this way?' (Matt. 26:54). Jesus had to follow His Father's plan: it involved His crucifixion, and He was not going to be diverted from it.

In fact, it goes further than that; Jesus reached out His hand to the very man whom Peter had just tried to kill. What would His touch involve? The touch of one whose divine power could command a storm to settle or put death into reverse. The amazing answer is that Jesus' touch would restore to physical wholeness the very individual charged with the task of taking forward the events which would culminate in His crucifixion. What an insight into the heart of the King, and how God's kingdom will truly come. It will come through the all-powerful, miracle-working, Son of God freely laying down His life in the place of sinners, including those who arrested Him.

I wonder what Malchus thought in the weeks that followed when he heard the news (the 'good news!') that Jesus had risen from the dead. Could he ignore the fact that he heard it with two ears and not one, and fail to be reminded of the willingness of Jesus to embrace the death of the cross?

Prophet, Priest and King

The President of the United States is generally considered to be the most powerful individual on the planet. Backed by the might of the world's largest economy, he sits at the apex of the political process in which he combines three distinct roles in one office. 'Mr President' is at one and the same time head of state, head of government and commander-in-chief of the armed forces. When the New Testament identifies Jesus of Nazareth as the promised Messiah (the Christ), it is describing a unique individual who in His person also combines three roles. Jesus is presented as the complete fulfilment of everything that the Old Testament pointed toward and as a result is everything the sinner needs.

Jesus is the perfect prophet

The task of any prophet was to reveal the mind of God and call people back to God. In that sense, we could say that Jesus is the prophet par excellence. But the New

Testament is not content with even that elevated description. Listen to the introduction to the Book of Hebrews:

> In the past God spoke to our ancestors through the prophets at many times and in various ways, but in these last days he has spoken to us by his Son, whom he appointed heir of all things, and through whom also he made the universe. The Son is the radiance of God's glory and the exact representation of his being, sustaining all things by his powerful word. After he had provided purification for sins, he sat down at the right hand of the Majesty in heaven.
> (Heb. 1:1-3)

The writer is telling us that while Jesus Christ follows on from the prophets, He is more than just another prophet. Jesus not only speaks for God but speaks as God. And because of who He is, He is now God's final 'message' to mankind. It is not just that Jesus, like the prophets before Him, pointed the way back to God. He alone could say, *I am the way* (John 14:6). There is an immeasurable distance between pointing the way to God, and actually being that way.

Jesus is the perfect priest

For well over a millennium Israel had observed its God-given sacrificial system. Day by day and year after year the blood of animals had been shed in recognition of the guilt of both individual and nation before a holy God. Standing between this offended God and a guilty people was the figure of the High Priest. All hope of forgiveness for sinners rested upon his mediation on their behalf before God. And the message of the New Testament is that the sinner need look no further, and dare look nowhere else, than to Jesus Christ:

'For there is one God and one mediator between God and mankind, the man Christ Jesus, who gave himself as a ransom for all people. ... ' (1 Tim. 2:5-6). Jesus Christ is the perfect

priest who secures forgiveness for the sinner, for the sacrifice He offered was that of Himself. As Jesus explained: *'For even the Son of Man did not come to be served, but to serve, and to give his life as a ransom for many.'* (Mark 10:45)

Jesus is the perfect king

Centuries before the birth of Jesus,
Isaiah prophesied of the coming Messiah:

> For to us a child is born, to us a son is given, and the government will be on his shoulders. And he will be called Wonderful Counsellor, Mighty God, Everlasting Father, Prince of Peace. Of the greatness of his government and peace there will be no end. He will reign on David's throne and over his kingdom …
>
> (Isa. 9:6-7)

If the hope held out in the Old Testament Scriptures was 'the King will come', the triumphant response of the New Testament is 'the King *has* come!' The question asked at His birth was, *'Where is the one who has been born king of the Jews?'* (Matt. 2:2). And the charge against Him for which He was crucified and that literally accompanied Him to His death (for Pilate had a notice prepared and fastened to the cross) read: *'JESUS OF NAZARETH, THE KING OF THE JEWS'* (John 19:19).

But we must understand that this king and His kingdom is unlike any other. When challenged by Pilate if He was indeed a king, Jesus answered, *'My kingdom is not of this world …'* (John 18:36). His kingdom was a heavenly kingdom, God's own kingdom, brought into our world. And ruling over this divine kingdom was not a king who would lord it over His subjects, to His advantage, but the humble Shepherd-King who instead, would give His life for His own (John 10:11). As countless Christians have discovered, His reign is neither heavy nor harsh:

Come unto me, all you who are weary and burdened, and I will give you rest. Take my yoke upon you and learn from me, for I am gentle and humble in heart, and you will find rest for your souls. For my yoke is easy and my burden is light.

(Matt. 11:28-30)

A final encounter: signposts for eternity

Two other men, both criminals, were also led out with him to be executed. When they came to the place called the Skull, they crucified him there, along with the criminals – one on his right, the other on his left. Jesus said, 'Father, forgive them, for they do not know what they are doing.' And they divided up his clothes by casting lots.

The people stood watching, and the rulers even sneered at him. They said, 'He saved others; let him save himself if he is God's Messiah, the Chosen One.'

The soldiers also came up and mocked him. They offered him wine vinegar and said, 'If you are the king of the Jews, save yourself.'

There was a written notice above him, which read: THIS IS THE KING OF THE JEWS.

One of the criminals who hung there hurled insults at him: 'Aren't you the Messiah? Save yourself and us!'

But the other criminal rebuked him. 'Don't you fear God,' he said, 'since you are under the same sentence? We are punished justly, for we are getting what our deeds deserve. But this man has done nothing wrong.'

Then he said, 'Jesus, remember me when you come into your kingdom.'

Jesus answered him, 'Truly I tell you, today you will be with me in paradise.'

(Luke 23:32-43)

Here's a remarkable thing: the Bible itself makes the claim that the death of the Son of God on a Roman cross will forever stand as the most significant moment in all of history and throughout eternity. And yet, in its own account of that momentous event, we are informed that there were three men who died on crosses that fateful day. It's as if the camera, which is focussed on Jesus, pans a little from side to side. What are we to make of that? Who were these other men the Word of God immortalised?

United in life

The first thing we can confidently say is that the significance of these men does not lie in who they were. We know nothing about their personal lives. We don't know their names, what age they were, where they came from, or whether they had families of their own. In fact we only know one thing about them and, to make sure we don't miss it, Luke repeats it four times. These men were criminals. In older translations of the Bible they are described as thieves. But that requires some explanation. Without wanting to minimise just how harsh the Romans could be in their application of the law of the land, they were not in the habit of crucifying men for acts of petty theft. Josephus, the first century Jewish historian, helps throw some light on this. He used the same word when referring to political activists prepared to kill in pursuit of their cause as Matthew uses to describe these thieves. The majority view is that these men were most likely bandits who viewed themselves as Robin Hood figures as they resisted Roman oppression by conducting raids against their supply-trains and officials. There is, however, one thing we can be quite sure about. Whatever the precise nature of their past activities, they were coming to a very public and painful end.

We are left with this picture. Both men were clearly lawbreakers (Category A 'sinners'), they were at the point of entering eternity, and found themselves (literally) separated by Christ in their death. We may not be far from the mark in concluding that the Word of God has preserved the account of their departures from this world so that we might learn from them, as those who will follow in the path of one or the other.

Divided in death

I find it particularly sad to read the account of the final hours of the first 'thief' Luke describes for us. Put simply, he had nothing but contempt for the individual at his side. Indeed, he pitched in with the mockery of the crowd, echoing their taunts, while adding a twist of his own, *'Save yourself **and us**!'* What nonsense it all was. The Messiah-King unable to save Himself, let alone His people! But what terrible irony is at work here, for supremely able though He was, the very reason the Chosen One was unwilling to save Himself was that He might provide salvation for all gathered around His cross, our abusive criminal included. As the camera pans away, we are left with nothing but the hopelessness of a Christ-rejecting death.

And yet, what a marvellous scene comes into view as our attention is directed to the other criminal. That may sound like a perverse statement to make; for, surely, the brutality was no less and death was just as certain? Yes, but this man was prepared to embrace his own desperation before God, and call upon Jesus as his only hope. And that made all the difference to the short time he had left in this world and, more importantly, how he entered the next. The 'penitent thief' faced reality as the enormity of his sin and the prospect of eternity stretched out before him. He 'feared God' and knew that he was completely unprepared to meet Him. As one who had traded in death himself, he accepted that death was now the just punishment for his deeds, and for those of his colleague. But he knew that what was true of them did not apply to the one who was suffering the same sentence on that central cross. He was utterly innocent for *'this man has done nothing wrong.'* Please take note of that: this dying man was just as convinced of Jesus' sinlessness as he was of his own sinfulness, and those are necessary steps on the path that leads to salvation.

The King's mercy

And his understanding didn't stop there. He had heard how the rulers and soldiers mimicked the claims and mocked the credentials of this Messiah-King. He had read the inscription nailed to His cross, identifying Him as King of the Jews. He could see the thorny symbol of royal ridicule they had pressed on His head. But, because he came to believe that this was precisely who hung beside him, he called out, *'Jesus, remember me when you come into your kingdom.'* Only one person has a kingdom and that is a king! The thief was not only convinced that this undeserved death was not the end for Jesus, but that a glorious future lay ahead of Him and he wanted to be part of it! With absolutely nothing to offer Him and with his only hope being this King's mercy, he invited Jesus to think on him *when* (not 'if ') that reign began. And in response he received the promise that millions since have taken into death with them, *'today you will be with me in paradise.'* He had no good works to offer and no contribution that he could make, yet he received the royal assurance that he would be with the King before the day had reached its end.

Divine disclosure

So here, truly, is a marvellous scene. Amidst all the horror and brutality of crucifixion we see, with such powerful clarity, where hope for hopeless sinners is found. It is found in the unearned mercy of the King of kings, who laid down His life that all who repent of their sin and call upon Him in faith may live in His presence for evermore.

Jesus reveals God perfectly. And the God He reveals is one who pursues sinners in grace. Jesus' mission was to seek and to save, not to search and destroy. He brought the message of the love of God to a world broken by sin. He shows us a God who we need not run from but whom we can turn to. Jesus reveals the very heart of God.

QUESTIONS FOR PERSONAL REFLECTION/GROUP DISCUSSION

1. Jesus said *'anyone who has seen me has seen the Father'* (John 14:9). What did He mean by that?

2. What did Jesus understand His mandate to be? What are the implications of this?

3. Why did the Pharisees largely reject Jesus while so many of the publicans (tax collectors) received Him? How is this still relevant to people today?

4. What does the miracle of the healing of Malchus reveal about Jesus?

5. How does Jesus 'fulfil' the roles of prophet, priest and King? Why does this bring hope and encouragement to us as sinners?

6. What do you think of Jesus' promise to the dying criminal, *'today you will be with me in paradise'*?

7. What stands out most for you from Jesus' public ministry? How does it help you understand God better?

Reason three

BECAUSE HE DIED FOR OUR SINS

I have a confession to make.

I'm no art expert. In fact, so much of the 'high culture' thing is wasted on me. If you mention Caravaggio, Giotto and Tintoretto, I am likely to turn on Sky Sports News to see which Premiership club has been active in the transfer market!

What the aforementioned gentlemen have in common, is that they all tried their hand at capturing on canvas the crucifixion of Jesus. And, in the case of their works, they have become priceless masterpieces. Giotto's attempt, for example, has been dated as early as the year 1290, and if it hung in your house, you wouldn't be leaving the door unlocked on the way out!

But I want to take you back much further than that. The particular piece of art that I want to share with you is actually the earliest known surviving representation of Jesus on the cross. Experts are divided on a precise date but all are agreed that it cannot be later than the third century.

Before we go any further, you may wish to see it for yourself. Simply search online 'Alexamenos drawing', but prepare to be underwhelmed!

Let me explain it to you.

This is a 'graffito'. That's not a word often used, but its plural form ('graffiti') is one we are all too familiar with. It was discovered in 1857 in a guardroom near to the Circus Maximus in Rome and is housed there today in the Palatine Museum. This 'wall-scratching' is actually an attempt at satire. I suppose it is the forerunner of the little cartoons that still find a place in the serious broadsheet newspapers today. The 'artist' has selected one of the controversial issues of his day in order to poke fun at a particular group within Roman society. The earliest pictorial representation of the crucifixion is essentially a cartoon with a caption.

Here is the scene.

A young man stands with his arm raised in worship to his god. The caption reads 'ALEXAMENOS SEBETE THEON', which translates as 'Alexamenos worships (his) god.' But here comes the joke, the jibe, the punch-line (look at the sketch again!) Who is his god? Well, for starters he is stretched out on a cross, but then notice that though he has the body of a human he has the head of a donkey!

This was no attempt borne of a sense of reverence to capture the horror of the crucifixion of Jesus. No! This was pure mockery and ridicule. And the object of derision was not only the 'god' on the cross, but also the fool who worshipped him!

Now I cannot speak with complete certainty about our cartoonist, but I'm pretty confident that the one thing he simply could not get his head around was this:

WHAT SORT OF GOD ENDS UP, AS A MAN, DYING ON A CROSS?

Actually, I think that is a really good question. And, as I will attempt to show, one the Bible was written to answer. The Bible really is the most amazing of books on so many levels. You don't have to be a Christian to see that it is unique both in terms of its circulation among us and its influence upon us. What many discover often to their surprise, when they start reading the Bible for themselves is the tremendous unity of this 'library' of books. Even though the Bible consists of sixty-six books, 1,189 chapters, 31,173 verses, and 773,692 words (depending on which version you are using), it tells *one story,* for it is the product of *one mind.* And this is all the more re-remarkable when you factor in that it was written over a period of approximately 1,600 years, in three different languages, by over forty different authors. However, what shocks people even more and that includes many in our modern and ever so savvy generation, is how it reaches us at the deepest level. It touches us at the core of who we are. It speaks to us with such clarity and authority that is beyond the merely human. We find in the Bible not the answer to all our questions but the solution to our greatest problem.

Now that last statement may amaze and annoy in equal measure. How can it be that the Bible offers the 'solution' to our greatest problem? As you read this you are maybe thinking that life is rather good; the Bible then can't have the solution because you can't see the problem! It is, however, worth persevering, for the Bible like a good doctor is honest enough to point out our condition even if *we* have missed the symptoms. And it is as we come to understand the message of the Bible that we also find the answer to the issue raised by our ancient cartoonist *what sort of god ends up, as a man, dying on a cross?*

Getting to grips with God!

In one sense I'm about to attempt the impossible. I am going to describe for you not only what God is like, but what He actually **IS** in Himself. And, to further impress you, I'm going to do it in a couple of three-word phrases! In case you're thinking that I have gone mad, I hasten to add that I will simply be quoting someone who has done it before me. Someone, in fact, who was inspired by God for that very purpose. Yet another wonderful thing about the Bible is how its truth can satisfy both the greatest intellect while remaining accessible even to a child.

God is Light
(1 John 1:5)
and
God is Love
(1 John 4:8)

There you have it! The apostle John is describing for us the very nature of God Himself. This is what the theologians would call God's essential being.

It is absolutely vital that we hear **both** these descriptions. Both are true and must be held together. We will have a distorted view of God if we see only half of what John has written. God is light, but He is not only light. God is love, but He is not only love.

God is light

From Genesis to Revelation the Bible is utterly insistent that God is absolutely pure and righteous in Himself. Whether Old or New Testament, the chorus is the same:

Holy, holy, holy is the LORD Almighty …

(Isa. 6:3)

… Holy, holy, holy is the Lord God Almighty, …

(Rev. 4:8)

The full version of what John wrote is, *'God is light; in him there is no darkness at all.'* The apostle Paul is in perfect agreement for he tells us of God *'who lives in unapproachable light.'* (1 Tim. 6:16). The writer to the Hebrews reminds his readers that *'our God is a consuming fire.'* (Heb. 12:29)

I suspect we get the picture. The image of pure and unrestrained light communicates to us the radiant holiness of God. There is an unapproachable and unbearable quality to it. And the problem does not lie with the one who is light, but with those who seek to stand before Him in that light. This is threatening news for people who are marked by the 'darkness' of unrighteousness and impurity.

Make no mistake about it, the Bible does teach that God's holiness is a problem for sinners. In fact, it is our most fundamental problem. It can never be an option for God who is light, to ignore sin or reach an accommodation with it. This truth has universal relevance, *'for **all** have sinned and fall short of the glory of God'* (Rom. 3:23). It is necessary for us to hear the 'bad news' of the Bible if we are to fully appreciate its good news. The bad news is that we are separated from a holy God on account of our sin. Worse, we are under His righteous condemnation on account of that sin. Worse still, we are destined for certain judgement as punishment for our sin.

How do you feel when you think about the holiness of God? Does it warm your heart? Does it draw you to Him? Not if you see yourself as a sinner!

When Peter gained a glimpse into the identity of Jesus, he fell on his face and begged Jesus to depart from him, for he knew he was a sinful man (Luke 5:8). A sinner's sense of guilt is the inevitable result of an insight into divine holiness. But it is a necessary journey to make, for we will never discover the truth about ourselves unless we are willing to face the truth about God:

> This is the verdict: light has come into the world, but men loved darkness instead of light because their deeds were evil. Everyone who does evil hates the light, and will not come into the light for fear that his deeds will be exposed.
>
> (John 3:19-20)

Maybe you think I am going too far, but it seems to me that the Bible judges us the moral equivalents of woodlice. Put it to the test. On a sunny day, lift that plant pot at the back of your house and watch woodlice do what woodlice do. They will immediately and instinctively set off in search of darkness. According to our verses, woodlice and sinners have a lot in common!

What am I saying? Is God's holiness a bad thing? Is it the unfortunate truth about God that we must (if reluctantly) swallow? Absolutely not! The point is that if God were *only* holy (light), then it would leave us as sinners forever condemned without a shred of hope.

But God is not only light.

God is love

From Genesis to Revelation the Bible insists that God is love. It is true to say that the *fulness* of the love of God is revealed in the New Testament, but God was never anything other than a God of love:

The Lord appeared to us in the past, saying:'I have loved you with an everlasting love; I have drawn you with unfailing kindness.

(Jer. 31:3)

How is it that God's loving nature is fully revealed in the New Testament? What happened that led to full disclosure of this truth?

The apostle Paul responds like this:

… God demonstrates his own love for us in this: while we were still sinners, Christ died for us.

(Rom. 5:8)

For Paul, there is objective, historical and irrefutable evidence of the love of God. And it is encountered in the sacrificial death of Jesus Christ. Through contemplating it we see into the heart of God!

This is in perfect agreement with what John wrote in his description of God:

… God is love. This is how God showed his love among us: he sent his one and only Son into the world that we might live through him. This is love: not that we loved God, but that he loved us and sent his Son as an atoning sacrifice for our sins.

(1 John 4:8-10)

This is who God is. Yes, He is absolutely holy in Himself. He is light. But because He is not only light, but also love, He has come to us in the person of His Son. And He came not as our judge to punish us, but as our saviour to rescue us. Without any love for Him on our part, Jesus came to offer Himself in our place and to answer for our sin. It is when we encounter the cross of Christ that we see the full glory of God who is both light and love.

The wonder of the cross

You will not find a Christian on earth (or in heaven!) who fully understands all that took place when the Son of God died in the place of sinners. The old hymn 'Give me a sight, O Saviour' expresses well our desire:

Oh, make me understand it,
Help me to take it in;
What it meant to thee, the Holy One,
To bear away my sin.

As you read some of the Bible's own commentary on the death of Christ, see how in that unique event God's holiness is satisfied and His love demonstrated:

For Christ also suffered once for sins, the righteous for the unrighteous, to bring you to God.

(1 Pet. 3:18)

Christ redeemed us from the curse of the law by becoming a curse for us, …

(Gal. 3:13)

God made him who had no sin to be sin for us, so that in him we might become the righteousness of God.

(2 Cor. 5:21)

It is because of the truth of those statements that Paul insists Christ is mankind's only hope. There is no other saviour:

… there is one God and one mediator between God and mankind, the man Christ Jesus, who gave himself as a ransom for all people.

(1 Tim. 2:5-6)

If Paul is sounding somewhat politically incorrect, I'm afraid Peter is no different:

> Salvation is found in no-one else, for there is no other name under heaven given to mankind by which we must be saved.
>
> (Acts 4:12)

Then again, Jesus Himself would appear to be the source of the problem of such exclusive claims:

> … I am the way and the truth and the life. No one comes to the Father except through me.
>
> (John 14:6)

I realise I have thrown a lot of texts at you but the reason for doing this is to show that the central message of the New Testament is that God has acted decisively through Jesus Christ.

It would be a tragedy of indescribable proportions to miss what God has done for us in sending His Son. There can be no better message for lost, fallen, guilty sinners than the cross of Christ. We can come to God and He will accept us if we come through His Son. Because of Jesus and His death on the cross God can be both *just* and the *justifier* of the sinner who has faith in Jesus (Rom. 3:26). God has been true to His holiness and His love, and both are seen in awesome harmony at Calvary.

Divine substitution

We are all familiar with the use of substitutes in the world of sport. If someone is having a bad game, or a change of tactics is required, or a player picks up an injury, the manager will tell the 'sub' to get warmed up. One player goes off and another comes on in his place. Somewhat embarrassingly, I have to admit I once played a football match in which we played the full 90 minutes with ten men while having a sub on the line. No, FIFA had not introduced some new regulation; rather, our master tactician of a manager had difficulty counting when it came to double digits. Better still, the aforementioned sub's occupation was that of government statistician! That's one post-match analysis session I'll never forget!

Calvary witnessed the ultimate substitution. The Christian writer John Stott expresses it wonderfully in his classic work, *The Cross of Christ*:

> The essence of sin is man substituting himself for God, while the essence of salvation is God substituting himself for man. Man asserts himself against God and puts himself where only God deserves to be; God sacrifices himself for man and puts himself where only man deserves to be. Man claims prerogatives that belong to God alone; God accepts penalties that belong to man alone. (p. 160)

Earlier in that same book he wrote:

> At the cross in holy love God through Christ paid the full penalty of our disobedience himself. He bore the judgement we deserve in order to bring us the forgiveness we do not deserve. On the cross divine mercy and justice were equally expressed and eternally reconciled. God's holy love was 'satisfied'. (p. 89)

'Do' or 'Done'

People sometimes confuse the good news of Jesus with religion. There is a simple way to distinguish between the two. With religion there is always some duty to discharge, some obligation to obey, some standard to achieve, or some contribution to make. There is always 'our part'. It was no coincidence that from the cross Jesus cried, *'It is finished'* (John 19:30). If Christ completed the work of securing forgiveness for sinners, it is not only unnecessary for us to try to achieve it for ourselves but the very attempt insults the sacrifice that made it possible. As Paul puts it, *'I do not set aside the grace of God, for if righteousness could be gained through the law* [our good works], *Christ died for nothing'* (Gal. 2:21). What irresistible logic. If we could have made it on our own then Christ's death was a terrible tragedy! We are not making a contribution to our acceptance by God when we come to him in an attitude of repentance for sin and trust in His Son. We are simply taking up His offer of a free and undeserved salvation.

Grace or Guilt

How any sinner responds to the cross of Christ is a matter of the ultimate importance. The Bible teaches that the preaching of the cross actually divides mankind into two camps. That makes perfect sense if we have understood what took place there. When people are confronted with the Christ of the cross, they make a choice. Either they are drawn to God and receive His gracious offer of forgiveness, or they turn away from God, adding the decisive sin of rejection to their previous offences. It was Jesus Himself who taught that the severest judgement is reserved for those who had the greatest opportunity to receive forgiveness yet chose to reject Him (Matt. 11:20-24). No one can claim to be neutral before the cross of Christ.

Speaking personally...

At the age of fourteen I had, what seemed to me, a major problem. Just at that self-conscious stage in my development, I had noticed that there was a flaw on this body beautiful of mine! Right at the centre of my chest there was what could only be described as a 'dent'. This imperfection had not escaped the notice of my classmates, and it became the subject of 'mature' discussion on a couple of occasions in the sports changing room. I decided that enough was enough and mentioned to my parents that my chest was different and asked if they could explain why! They could not (having failed to notice it!) but pacified me by making an appointment with the family doctor. Upon examination the doctor was able to label my abnormality. I had a contracted sternum bone and it had been that way from birth. He carried out a simple breathing test and told me that it was having no impact whatsoever on me physically. To be honest, I knew that already. My issue lay with the 'social' consequences of my condition!

The outcome was that the doctor referred me to a surgeon at the Royal Victoria Hospital, Belfast, who could perform a cosmetic procedure on my body. That sounded just fine, I thought, and on the first morning of my summer holidays my little suitcase was packed and off I went to hospital but that same afternoon events headed in a rather unexpected direction. The surgeon scheduled for theatre the next day dropped in to talk me through what lay ahead. He began by telling me that I would have a steel pin in my chest for the next six months and would not be able to play any sport. Then, after the six months, he would operate again to remove the pin. Next, he explained how I would – quite literally – be tied to the ceiling for the next five days. I would be raised via a pulley system which would help me with breathing and clearing my lungs. Yes, you probably are asking what was I thinking of! The clincher, however, was still to come: I was informed that I would be left with a scar running ten inches long and six inches wide radiating out from the centre of my chest. The surgeon smiled knowingly at me as he left saying 'See you in the morning young man!'

I suspect it will not come as a major surprise to learn that when my father came up to visit me that night he found his son sitting on his bed fully dressed with suitcase packed. I cannot even remember the process of signing out … I was out of there as quickly as I could go.

Basically, I did the maths. Was I going to be any better off with a cross on my chest in exchange for my dent?

Exactly one year later, on the first day of the summer holidays, I set off with a group of friends to Paris. To this day I still don't know how I got my parents to agree to it. I had just turned fifteen that same week and this was my first experience of doing my own thing on holiday. We hadn't even reached Stranraer by boat before I had managed to secure and consume a supply of alcohol. What plans I had for the next seventeen days! What new opportunities lay in front of me free of any adult supervision!

But there was one opportunity I just hadn't seen coming.

It soon became clear that the guy who had organised the trip (a seventeen year old student!) was a Christian. For the first time in my life someone sat down with me and shared the good news of Jesus Christ. He explained to me that we couldn't make ourselves right with God and that we didn't need to try either because Jesus was the way to God. Because of His death on the cross, sinners could be forgiven and enter into a personal relationship with God. Without fear of contradiction, I can say that this simply astounded me. I had no problem accepting I was a sinner and neither did anyone else who knew me! I can vividly recall making my way to the hotel toilet so that I could be alone – and it was there that I asked God to save me and invited Jesus Christ into my life.

One year earlier I had fled at the prospect of having a cross on my chest for the rest of my days. Now, in a hotel toilet in Paris, I had a cross branded on my heart that has changed me forever. The truth of the love of God for me as a sinner has become the ultimate reality in my life. Along with every other Christian, I now know that nothing *'will be able to separate us from the love of God which is in Christ Jesus our Lord'* (Rom. 8:39).

QUESTIONS FOR PERSONAL REFLECTION/GROUP DISCUSSION

1. What is your reaction to the Alexamenos drawing?

2. How does the biblical description of God as 'light' convey what He is like? What are the implications of this for us?

3. How do we see both God's holiness and His love in perfect harmony at the cross?

4. Why do you think a religion based on rules and regulations is appealing to many people?

5. 'The essence of sin is man substituting himself for God, while the essence of salvation is God substituting himself for man' (John Stott, on p. 64). How do you feel about both parts of this statement?

6. If we are able to make our own way to Him, why would God have sent His Son into the world? What happens to the cross if we can establish our own righteousness before God?

7. What does the cross say to anyone who wants to know if God loves them? How do Romans 5:8 and 1 John 4:9-10 help with this?

Reason four

BECAUSE HE ROSE AGAIN FROM THE DEAD

The curious case of George Wilson

George Wilson has gone down in American legal history as the first man who refused to accept a pardon. In 1829, Wilson along with an accomplice robbed a mail carrier and 'put the life of the carrier in jeopardy' in the process. Both men were condemned to death for their deeds. Indeed, Wilson's partner in crime was hanged soon after the sentence was handed down by the court. Through the intervention of some powerful and well placed friends, however, Wilson escaped execution. President Andrew Jackson exercised his presidential prerogative and issued a pardon. The sentence of death was commuted to twenty years' imprisonment.

Amazingly Wilson refused to accept the pardon, with the result that the issue was raised for the first time in the American legal system:

DOES A PARDON CARRY FORCE IF IT IS NOT ACCEPTED?

Can someone be forced to be pardoned? It fell to the Supreme Court to rule on the matter and you can read its full and lengthy judgement online (simply search 'George Wilson pardon'). The answer was an emphatic '**NO**'. The key statement in their ruling was:

> A pardon, which is an act of grace, carries no force unless it is accepted by the individual to whom it is offered.

George Wilson persisted in his refusal to accept the pardon and thus went to the gallows in 1833.

He is risen (! or ?)

We are about to embark upon a consideration of the resurrection of Jesus Christ. This will necessarily involve us interacting with the main objections brought against it. Even in a brief chapter like this, it will require thoughtful analysis and argument. The danger is that it could appear as some sort of detached historical detective-style exercise. Engaging enough in itself, but hardly relevant to us today. That would be a dreadful miscalculation. Whether or not Jesus of Nazareth came out of the tomb really does matter. The New Testament teaches that God's pardon for sinners is inextricably bound up with the risen Christ. It goes so far as to say to Christians: *'… if Christ has not been raised, your faith is futile; you are still in your sins'* (1 Cor. 15:17). By raising Jesus from the dead, God has expressed His complete satisfaction with the sacrifice of His Son at Calvary.

There are really two issues at stake when we think about the resurrection of Jesus. Naturally enough, the first is: did it happen? And, let's be clear, if it didn't then Christ has nothing to offer – for He cannot then bring forgiveness from sin. The Bible itself spells that out. Are there really good reasons for believing that Jesus is alive right now? We just cannot afford *not* to think seriously about this issue. There is too much riding on it. And yet, even if after examining the evidence and being convinced that Jesus of Nazareth 'conquered the grave', there remains something to be decided upon: 'Will I personally come to Him in honest acknowledgement of my sin and with the desire to be free from it? Will I actually claim the pardon that He has won for me? Or, will I like George Wilson, refuse the grace extended to me and reject the pardon on offer?' That is a question that involves more than our understanding. That is a matter of the *heart.*

The central claim of the Christian faith is that Jesus rose again. It is also the most contested claim. Down through the centuries there have been many who have sought to refute the resurrection and have put forward their explanations for what really happened that first Easter. We can't look at all the alternatives but we can consider the best and most widely accepted of them. I will attempt to reproduce these views as fairly as possible.

The Four Gospels

Sometimes it will be obvious that the various denials of the resurrection simply go against logic and common sense. They just don't add up and you don't have to be a Christian to find them impossible to accept. In each and every case, however, these views contradict the biblical accounts of Matthew, Mark, Luke and John. In place of these *eye-witness accounts*, critics offer their own reconstructions. Do remember the Gospels were written and circulated in the lifetimes of the people and authorities mentioned in them. They gained acceptance in the very region where the events they recorded took place. They were written in a climate of hostility by individuals who were not expecting to receive gain but were willing to pay the price of telling the truth. It is an unassailable fact that the four Gospels remain the most scrutinized and verified documents in all of history. Perhaps the wisest thing to do is to read them (again?) for yourself. Do they read like the work of someone fabricating a falsehood? Do they read like the grief-induced delusions of heart-broken disciples? Or do they read like straightforward accounts of what actually happened when Jesus undid death and proved Himself to be the Son of God? (Rom. 1:4)

Buffers against engagement

I have to be honest and say that I meet more than a few individuals who do not even get to the stage of thinking seriously about the resurrection of Jesus. As soon as they sense they are within range of encountering it, their mental shutters come down. The two most common expressions of this refusal to engage are very different from each other but deliver the same outcome.

It didn't happen

The first is what I call the 'head in the sand' approach. It's not a very sophisticated approach and it is really the result of a lack of desire to discover the truth. It runs along these lines:

> I don't believe a word of it. The whole thing's made up. It's all just some fairy tale from the past. We don't even know if Jesus really existed, never mind rose again from the dead. It's nonsense from start to finish. It's nothing but kids' stuff!

That really will not do. Try telling the following first-century historians that Jesus never existed and was not reported to have risen from the dead. One is Jewish

(Josephus A.D. 37-100) and the other is Roman (Tacitus A.D. 56-117). *Both* were opponents of Christianity. Josephus records:

> Now there was about this time Jesus, a wise man, if it be lawful to call him a man; for he was a doer of wonderful works, a teacher of such men as receive the truth with pleasure. He drew over to him both many of the Jews and many of the Gentiles. He was (the) Christ. And when Pilate, at the suggestion of the principal men amongst us, had condemned him to the cross, those that loved him at the first did not forsake him; for he appeared to them alive again the third day; as the divine prophets had foretold these and ten thousand other wonderful things concerning him. And the tribe of Christians, so named from him, are not extinct at this day.
>
> (Josephus, *Antiquities of the Jews*, 18.64)

The scholarly consensus is that Josephus may not have been quite as enthusiastic about Jesus as these comments would indicate. But at the very least they provide solid confirmation that Jesus lived, died and was reported to have risen again from the dead.

The Roman senator and historian Tacitus was no friend of Christianity but he could not ignore its impact even at the heart of the empire. To his annoyance this 'mischievous superstition' not only survived the death of its founder but actually continued to spread. Tacitus writes:

> ... Nero fastened the guilt and inflicted the most exquisite tortures on a class hated for their abominations, called Christians by the populace. Christus, from whom the name had its origin, suffered the extreme penalty during the reign of Tiberius at the hands of one of our procurators, Pontius Pilate, and a most mischievous superstition, thus checked for a moment, again broke out in Judea, the first source of the evil, but even in Rome ...
>
> (Tacitus, *Annals*, 15.44)

If you disliked Christians as much as Tacitus did, you would have delighted to point out that the one whom they worshipped never existed. Facts, however, got in the way, Rome itself had executed Him!

To deny the historicity of Jesus and His death on the cross is just not a credible position. He is no fictional or mythological character. And the Christian claim is that this real person actually died and rose again and as a result has changed millions of lives. Surely that claim is worth investigating.

It couldn't happen

The second buffer against engagement with the truth of the resurrection is very different in character, but it produces the same result. This time the starting point is not the result of intellectual laziness but quite the reverse. People who view themselves as clear-thinking, rational, logical, scientifically-minded individuals come to the question of whether or not Jesus rose again from the dead like this:

> It's a non-starter! There is absolutely no point spending one moment of my time thinking about it for the reason it didn't happen is simply because it couldn't happen. It is impossible. The laws of science show that it is impossible for a dead body to come back to life again. Matter closed!

Stop the bus! If we are going to object to the resurrection of Christ on the grounds of science, then let's be good scientists. Let's be careful concerning what we claim for the laws of science. The fact is that the laws of science do not *make* anything happen. For example, it is not the law of gravity that makes an apple fall to the ground, but gravity itself. The law is a description of how gravity works based on observation. It describes how gravity observably works. But, as many scientists freely admit, the laws of science only tell us what happens as long as there is no interference from the outside. It is only if you assume that our universe is a closed system, *that it is all there is,* that something 'miraculous' like the resurrection becomes an impossibility. And that is not a conclusion drawn from science; it is a conviction of faith.

The true test of whether or not there has been interference from the outside in our world is not science; it is history. Is there credible evidence to show that there has been a direct intervention going against everything we have seen and come to expect? Of course, if there is a creator God, who stepped into our world in the person of Jesus Christ for the purposes of redemption, then the resurrection of Christ is not impossible in any way. In fact, by this unique event He would demonstrate powerfully and precisely just who He was.

So, beware those buffers against engagement. Don't be lazy and bury your head in the sand, *examine the evidence.* And don't overstretch science and say it is impossible, *examine the evidence.*

The resurrection of Jesus – three options

No-one can argue with the statement that unbelievers have had almost 2,000 years in which to contest the resurrection and provide alternative understandings of what really happened in the city of Jerusalem all those years ago. It is also true to say that even if a thousand different explanations are put forward to account for the events of the first Easter, we can hang each of them on one of three hooks:

1. An honest mistake was made
2. A deliberate fraud was perpetrated
3. The ultimate miracle occurred

By concentrating on the first two categories, we may discover that the third option fits the facts at every turn.

An honest mistake was made

It is only fair to say that most of the explanations put forward to disprove the resurrection suggest that no harm was intended. There was an initial misunderstanding which, regrettably, spread rapidly among simple folk who swallowed it completely. It's now all a bit embarrassing for us twenty-first century sophisticates. But let's not question the integrity of the people who believed in Jesus' resurrection; it's just their intelligence that is suspect.

Here are, in my opinion, the top four alternatives.

Swoon theory

This arose in the context of eighteenth-century rationalism. There was no resurrection for this simple reason, Jesus didn't die! Oh, everyone thought He had died but He had actually fainted. He 'swooned' from exhaustion, temporarily slipping into a state of shock, and to all intents and purposes He appeared dead. And so death-like was His condition, He was buried alive. But the following evening, in the cool air of the tomb, filled with the aroma of the burial spices, He revived (resuscitated) and left the tomb. When later Jesus appeared to His followers they jumped to the conclusion that He had risen from the dead.

I wonder if you feel that this has even a hint of plausibility about it. If so, then you need to factor in the following:

- Jesus had been abused by a large company of Roman soldiers

- He had been subjected to a Roman scourging (which on occasion caused prisoners to die)

- He had endured the horrors of crucifixion for six hours without any form of pain relief

- He had a Roman spear thrust into His side for the precise purpose of determining whether He was alive or not (this having been ordered by Pilate himself)

- The burial party confirmed that Jesus was dead and encased His body (mummy-style) in an estimated 100 pounds of spices

- His tomb was secured by a boulder which could not have weighed less than one tonne

- A Roman guard was stationed at His tomb to deter any interference with the burial site

- Having overcome all of this, Jesus somehow made His way through the streets of Jerusalem, located His followers and convinced them that He was alive and well!

I have to say that I find that more than a little hard to accept!

Let me add this: in all of documented history there is only one recorded occasion where an individual survived crucifixion. Josephus recounts that three men, known to him personally, were crucified at the same time. The crucifixion was just underway when Josephus witnessed their plight and immediately appealed to his friend Titus. News of a pardon was promptly relayed to the Roman official overseeing the executions. Despite receiving expert medical attention, only one of the men survived. That was without the beating by the soldiers, the scourging, six hours on a cross, piercing with a spear, actual burial, a sealed tomb, a guarded tomb …

Wrong tomb theory

The women turned up at the wrong tomb and thus jumped to the wrong conclusion. I like to call it the 'silly women' theory! Actually it involves a lot more 'silly' people than the small group of women who were first on the scene at the empty tomb.

The theory runs along these lines. So blinded by their grief, the women became confused as to the exact whereabouts of Jesus' burial. After all, one rock tomb looks just like another! And you need to keep in mind it was dusk when Jesus was being buried. In their grief and confusion, what the women actually came upon was an empty tomb alright, but the reason it was empty was because it was unused. It was all a case of 'tomb-trickery'.

How does that hold up under examination?

- Here is the only information that we have regarding these women and the burial of Jesus: *'they sat opposite the tomb'* (Matt. 27:61); they *'saw where he was laid'* (Mark 15:47); they *'saw the tomb and how his body was laid in it'* (Luke 23:55).

- This was a private burial ground. In fact, it was the reserved tomb of Joseph of Arimathea, a rich man and member of the influential Sanhedrin. Indeed, the burial took place in the tomb of one member of the Sanhedrin, with the cooperation of another member (Nicodemus). And the whole operation was officially approved by the Roman governor (Pilate). The detail is given in John's Gospel (19:38-42). Try missing that tomb!

- It would have been impossible to mistake the correct tomb for another reason. It had a Roman guard stationed there. Matthew records: '[the authorities] *went and made the tomb secure by putting a seal on the stone and posting the guard'* (27:66). This meant that a cord was stretched across the boulder blocking the tomb which was then 'sealed' at both sides with clay. Stamped into the clay was the signet of the Roman Governor. The punishment for breaking a Roman seal was death!

- So the tomb was well-known, the burial supervised, and the site officially sealed and guarded. But the women still got it wrong! Well, actually, everybody got it wrong. Peter and John must have gone to the wrong tomb as well. More than that, the Jewish authorities and the Roman authorities must also have turned up at the wrong location. They could have stopped the rumour of resurrection in a heartbeat by simply breaking the seal on the right tomb and *producing the body.*

Hallucination theory
It's probably true to say that this is the most popular 'natural' explanation.

It goes something like this. The followers of Jesus were absolutely devastated by His death. They had invested in Him heavily but now all their hopes lay buried with Him in the grave. And in that heartbroken, emotionally unstable, psychologically vulnerable state, they imagined that the one they missed so much was still with them. What they mistook for reality was just the heart playing a trick on the mind.

How does that stand up?

The first thing we must do is set this theory alongside analysis from the fields of psychiatry and psychology with regard to hallucinations. It is not an exaggeration to say that everything about these so-called hallucinations goes against the findings of mental health professionals:

- Only particular types of people experience hallucinations which have not been induced by drugs. They are normally paranoid or schizophrenic individuals. Are we to conclude that the vast number of eye-witnesses *all* suffered from mental illness?

- Hallucinations are notoriously individualistic. No two persons undergo exactly the same phenomena. Only two of the documented resurrection appearances were to individuals. The others were to groups, or in one case, to a crowd of more than 500 (1 Cor. 15:6).

- The appearances of Jesus emphasised physical reality. This is overwhelmingly not the case with hallucinations. Christ invited touch. He actually ate with His disciples. This was not the appearance of some disembodied spirit.

- These 'hallucinations' not only happened to lots of different people, but they occurred at different times of the day, in different places, to people doing different things. Again, this is precisely the reverse of the norm for hallucinations.

- These 'hallucinations' are said to have been the result of the disciples not just longing but actually expecting to see Jesus. Nothing could be further from the truth. The women went to embalm the body. The disciples thought, at first, that Jesus was a spirit. Thomas cynically refused to believe Jesus was alive and demanded proof. The psychological state of the disciples was not expectation of Jesus' resurrection but resignation to His death.

- The fifteen or so hallucinations (appearances!) occurred within a definite forty-day period and then stopped abruptly and were not repeated. Hallucinations tend to dog people with mental illness all their days if treatment with drugs is not available.

If anyone chooses to believe that what happened that first Easter was some mass experience of hallucination, they need to be aware that this scenario is in conflict with everything that the professional world of mental health treatment has observed. And one unanswerable question remains: *why did the authorities not simply produce the body?* That would have brought an immediate end to any talk of resurrection. The authorities held all the cards, as long as they held the body.

Misunderstanding 'myth' theory

This pops up from time to time as some controversial bishop or theologian hits the headlines. It can be a bit confusing, for often it will be said that Jesus did rise again from the dead, but only in a 'spiritual' sense. In reality, His body remained in the grave and His followers knew that. But to express the fact that Jesus lived on in their hearts, and was not defeated by death, they constructed a myth. The New Testament writers freely composed their resurrection accounts with lots of colourful detail but all they were ever really saying was that Jesus lives on so long as we continue to acknowledge Him.

- Whilst it may cause initial confusion when this view is expressed by someone who appears to be associated with the Christian faith, it rapidly falls apart under examination. The simple fact is that there is absolutely no evidence whatsoever to support this theory. It cannot point to anything in history to sustain it. All the available evidence is against it.

- It is almost amusing (if it were not so serious) to hear what the New Testament writers actually say about the use of 'myth'. It is there in print for all to see. The apostle Peter wrote that the apostles did **not** follow *'cleverly invented stories'* (he uses the Greek word for myths) when they spoke of Christ, but were *'eye-witnesses'* of His majesty (see 2 Pet. 1:16). How could anyone think that Paul did not consider the bodily resurrection of Jesus as all-important after reading 1 Corinthians 15?

A deliberate fraud was perpetrated

We are coming now to more sinister material. To accuse the first-century believers of being fools is one thing; to charge them with deliberate deception is another.

Several theories have arisen which try to take account of the fact that the tomb of Jesus was clearly empty. Some have alleged that grave robbers were responsible for the removal of the body. If that be the case, then they must go down in history as the most incompetent or unsuccessful robbers of all time. They managed to make off with the worthless corpse, while leaving behind the expensive spices and valuable grave clothes! Others have alleged that either the Jewish or Roman authorities, for whatever reason, removed the body. Surely that would be the most self-defeating action in history. More to the point, all they had to do to squash the rumour of resurrection and forever put the record straight was produce the body or at least explain its whereabouts. These views hardly merit serious attention.

Undoubtedly the most serious and popular deception theory is that the disciples of Jesus stole the body. The post-execution situation is recreated like this.

Such was the devastation felt by the disciples of Jesus, having left all to follow Him, they collectively came up with a scam which would allow them to save face and continue as leaders in this popular movement. So the disciples executed a daring raid, staged a resurrection scene and disposed of the body of Jesus. And they succeeded, continuing to occupy positions of leadership for years to come knowing full well it was all built upon a phenomenal deception.

The logical inconsistencies of this view are staggering. Interestingly, it is the most ancient of all anti-resurrection theories and is even mentioned in the New Testament itself (see Matt. 28:11-15):

- It was the *Jewish authorities* (not the disciples) who hatched the deception! Faced with the humiliating news that Jesus had risen from the dead, they moved swiftly to put their version of events in place. The guards at the tomb, for whom the punishment for falling asleep on duty was death, were assured that they would be protected if they stuck with the story. They were given a sizable bribe for their trouble. But you would not have needed expert legal training to spot the weakness in their version of events: *'The disciples came and stole the body of Jesus while we slept'*. People who are sleeping tend to fare pretty poorly as eyewitnesses! And are we to believe that all of these trained soldiers nodded off at the same time?

- And just where did these death-defying disciples come from? They certainly weren't men like that a couple of days earlier when the soldiers seized Jesus and took Him away. Then, they all fled. In their own writings they openly confessed that after Jesus was executed they were to be found behind locked doors *'for fear of the Jews'*. Yet we are asked to accept that they were prepared to engage with trained soldiers, break an official seal and thus commit a capital crime, so they could deceive people with their lie!

- Here's another remarkably strange thing. These same men had increasingly been exposed to the ultimate standards of morality as they accompanied Jesus throughout His period of ministry. But now they are prepared to unleash the most wicked deception that the world has ever witnessed. And, they stick to it throughout their subsequent years without any qualms of conscience as they continue to teach the importance of honesty, integrity and truth to their followers.

- This really is the clincher; these deceivers got to enjoy the spoils of their deception! They would stand by and watch as countless numbers of their duped followers were ridiculed, persecuted and even martyred. What incredibly ruthless men they must have been as they kept silent and refused to call time on their dreadful deception. And, of course, we know from church history that ten of the eleven apostles were themselves martyred for their consistent preaching that Christ was raised from the dead. Not one recanted. Not one attempted to strike a deal with the executing authority in return for admitting it was all a lie. Men will die for something they believe to be true, *not for something they know to be a lie.*

Taking stock

It is important to understand that what we have been working through in these last few pages is the best that men have come up with to explain away the resurrection of Jesus Christ. Is the claim that Jesus has risen from the dead really all down to a misunderstanding among Jesus' followers? You have been confronted with the fatal flaws in the various scenarios that have been put forward. Are you prepared to believe that it was all some great conspiracy masterminded and executed by Jesus' deceitful disciples? Does that view have anything to commend it? I think the Christian author Josh McDowell summed it up well when he wrote: 'The difficulties of belief are great; the absurdities of unbelief are greater'.

It would be possible to work through the New Testament resurrection accounts and demonstrate how the resurrection of Jesus fits the facts of the first Easter and logically explains the actions of everyone caught up in the situation. But in the absence of any other possible explanation, perhaps we can move on to consider the implications for us of a living Christ.

The ultimate miracle occurred

The Bible tells us that the resurrection of Jesus Christ is great news for sinners who live their lives under the sentence of death. Death became part of the human experience as the result of sin and has a legitimate claim upon every individual 'born of Adam's race' (Rom. 5:12). In fact, we all move through this life in a state of spiritual death (separation from God) as we head inexorably towards our physical death. Paul reminds his fellow-Christians of the reality of their situation before they trusted in Christ: *'As for you, you were dead in your transgressions and sins'* (Eph. 2:1). But Jesus came into our world and changed everything! Though He was *fully* human, He was not *merely* human. He was the perfect Son of God who became the first man to live a life completely free of sin. And yet, He submitted to death, which had no claim upon him. He chose to pay a debt He did not owe, and that meant He died a death He had not earned. The amazing truth at the heart of the good news of Jesus is that He laid down his life and experienced death in the sinner's place.

Now this explains why the resurrection is all-important. It is the vindication of Jesus Christ as the true saviour of men. It demonstrates that God has accepted Christ's death in the place of the sinner. He has fully absorbed the penalty of God's broken law and the righteous wrath of God has been satisfied. Death is vanquished. The Puritan writer, John Owen, entitled his classic work on the cross-work of Jesus, 'The death of death in the death of Christ.' Death itself has received a death-blow! There is a man-sized hole in death produced by the risen Christ. An Easter poster picturing the empty tomb of Jesus captured it perfectly:

'Not a hopeless end ... but an endless hope!'

Who other than Jesus, the death-defeating Son of God, could say: '... *I am the resurrection and the life. The one who believes in me will live even though they die; and whoever lives by believing in me will never die* ...' (John 11:25). For the sinner who receives Christ, the reality of spiritual death is replaced by the presence of eternal life, and the fear associated with physical death is evicted by hope. Because Jesus lives we shall live also (John 14:19).

I won't be telling you anything you don't know when I say that people don't like to think or talk about death. 'What funeral preparations have you made?' is not in my experience the most welcome topic of conversation! And no matter which celebrity they use, those funeral payment plan advertisements, counselling us to be considerate and 'leave everything in order' for our loved ones, haven't inspired me to reach for the phone. Not even with the promise of a free Parker pen! Well, I want to share with you one detail of my funeral arrangements that I've already decided upon. That is the choice of the following hymn (Christians tend to sing this hymn on Easter Sunday so it will take some of them by surprise if I'm buried on one of the other 364 days!):

Thine be the glory, risen conquering Son;
Endless is the victory, Thou o'er death hast won;
Angels in bright raiment rolled the stone away;
Kept the folded grave clothes, where Thy body lay.
Thine be the glory, risen conquering Son;
Endless is the victory, Thou o'er death hast won.

Lo! Jesus meets us, risen from the tomb;
Lovingly He greets us, scatters fear and gloom;
Let the Church with gladness, hymns of triumph sing;
For her Lord now liveth, death hath lost its sting.
Thine be the glory, risen conquering Son;
Endless is the victory, Thou o'er death hast won.

No more we doubt Thee, glorious Prince of life;
Life is naught without Thee, aid us in our strife;
Make us more than conquerors, through Thy deathless love;
Bring us safe through Jordan, to Thy home above.
Thine be the glory, risen conquering Son;
Endless is the victory, Thou o'er death hast won.

There is hope for every sinner in this. The cross is bare; the tomb is empty; the throne of God is occupied! The conqueror of death is enthroned in heaven. And so it is written: '*...because Jesus lives for ever ... he is able to save* *completely those who come to God through him, because he always lives to intercede for them'* (Heb. 7:24-25).

QUESTIONS FOR PERSONAL REFLECTION/GROUP DISCUSSION

1. How important is the resurrection of Jesus to the Christian faith? Read 1 Corinthians 15:14-19. How does this affect your answer?

2. Does science rule out the possibility of Jesus having risen from the dead? If Jesus is who He claimed to be, the Son of God come into our world, how does this affect your answer?

3. Did you find any of the theories that deny the resurrection convincing?

4. How likely is it that Jesus' followers were involved in some sort of resurrection scam?

5. What other objections, if any, are there that were not covered in the chapter?

6. What is the relationship between Jesus' resurrection and His death on the cross?

7. In what ways does Jesus' resurrection give hope to the sinner who trusts in Him?

BECAUSE HE IS THE APPOINTED JUDGE

A tale of two brothers

As I write these words, I have in front of me two books which can be found side by side in any serious bookshop. There are two reasons for this. One is that both books deal with the same subject. The other is that the authors share the same family name. And the reason this is the case is no coincidence but is due to the fact that the two authors are brothers. It is ironic that you can find the books in such close proximity on the shelf, because you could not imagine a greater distance between the two viewpoints presented within the books.

Christopher Hitchens, who died in December 2011, aged 62, was a writer, journalist and popular public speaker. As a vicious opponent of belief in God and any form of organised religion, he became a high profile spokesperson for atheism. He was often interviewed on television warning of the dangers of religiously-inspired influence in the political arena or public space. His best-seller was published in 2007 and its title is as unambiguous as its content:

God is Not Great: How Religion Poisons Everything

Obviously the title plays on the Islamic phrase 'Allahu Akbar', translated as 'God is great', which for many in our world has become associated with acts of terrorism by extremists, and particularly with suicide bombers in the moment before detonation. It should be noted, however, that Christopher Hitchens' hostility is by no means restricted to Islamic fundamentalism. Indeed, he writes with unmistakable fury against the 'evils' of Christian instruction of the young.

But what of our second author?
Peter Hitchens is Christopher's younger brother by two and a half years. In common with his late brother, he is a journalist, historian, political commentator and author. The title of his best-seller will illustrate where the brothers parted company:

The Rage Against God: How Atheism Led Me To Faith

In his mind Peter is just as convinced of the bankruptcy of atheism as Christopher is in his of the danger of religion. At the very least this is an intriguing story of how two intelligent and articulate brothers, raised and educated in the same way, came to two staggeringly opposed worldviews and understandings of reality. What makes it more fascinating again is that Peter, as a young adult, believed passionately in an atheistic approach to life. However, it is what made the difference and helped bring him to not only reject atheism, but to embrace Christianity, that interests me. Helpfully Peter has mapped out his journey, not only in his book but also in an article published in his blog on 'MailOnline' which is available on the web 'How I found God and peace with my atheist brother'.

In an act of great symbolism, fifteen year-old Peter attempted to set fire to his Bible on the playing fields of his Cambridge boarding school. It all proved rather anti-climactic as the Bible mounted a stubborn defence and his friends gradually lost interest, drifting away one by one. But it was the thought that counted. He had come of age and was now ready to publicly reject the superstitions that had surrounded him in his youth. And, why not, for atheism made sense! Everything could now be explained and there was no legitimate place left in the universe for God.

The next fifteen years of Peter's life were shaped by the outworking of his embrace of atheism. But as Peter entered his thirties, something happened which ultimately brought his atheistic thought-world crashing down around him and he just did not see it coming.

When on holiday in Burgundy, Peter noticed in a guidebook that a famous painting by Rogier van der Weyden could be viewed near to where he was staying. The painting was called 'Last Judgement'. Initially he scoffed at the prospect but later decided to go and see it anyway. What followed is best told in his own words:

> … I gaped, my mouth actually hanging open, at the naked figures fleeing toward the pit of Hell. These people did not appear remote or from the ancient past; they were my own generation. Because they were naked, they were not imprisoned in their own age by time-bound fashions … They were me, and people I knew…I had absolutely no doubt that I was among the damned, if there were any damned. Van der Weyden was still earning his fee, nearly 500 years after his death.

Peter Hitchens had tried for years to bury the reality of God beneath his atheism. But fear of judgement, and the prospect of being lost forever, broke through his defences and forced him to examine the atheistic assumptions upon which he had built his life. It was for this reason that he subtitled his book: 'How atheism led me to faith'. Peter discovered he had, along with so many of his contemporaries, believed a lie.

Now I realize that in this age it is deeply unpopular to speak of a day of judgement in which sinners will be held to account for their sins and face the eternal consequences of those sins. But the Bible will not sanction such silence. More than that, it insists that responsibility for the task of judgement falls squarely upon the shoulders of Jesus Christ. He is the appointed Judge.

The Day of Judgement

Many people have their own ideas for what the Day of Judgement will be like. Or perhaps it would be more accurate to say that many have their preference for what it should be like. The image of an individual standing before God is still a permissible concept if we are talking about a 'monster[who murdered children, or some sadistic general who presided over 'ethnic cleansing'. Few would shed tears at the prospect of such individuals spending a very long time in some version or other of hell. But that is as far as it goes. The general consensus appears to be that the Day of Judgement is fine so long as we are thinking about the Hitlers of this world. And, of course, we reassure ourselves, 'I'm no Hitler!'

But what does the Bible actually say about the Day of Judgement? Surely this is too important an issue to just go by what we feel would be appropriate, or by what others say will happen. Surely we owe it to ourselves to at least understand the picture presented in the Bible?

And Christians cannot shirk their responsibility to teach truthfully on this sombre matter; no matter how unpalatable or unpopular the message of judgement to modern tastes, they are called to be messengers and not editors of the truth.

> Then I saw a great white throne and him who was seated on it. The earth and the heavens fled from his presence, and there was no place for them. And I saw the dead, great and small, standing before the throne, and books were opened. Another book was opened, which is the book of life. The dead were judged according to what they had done as recorded in the books. The sea gave up the dead that were in it, and death and Hades gave up the dead that were in them, and each person was judged according to what they had done. Then death and Hades were thrown into the lake of fire. The lake of fire is the second death. Anyone whose name was not found written in the book of life, he was thrown into the lake of fire.
>
> (Rev. 20:11-15)

That is the fullest account that the Bible gives us of the Day of Judgement for sinners. It may be brief but it is no less solemn for it. The apostle John was inspired by God to record the key information that we need to know about this day of days. There are five characteristics of the Day of Judgement that are worth noting.

It is INESCAPABLE

Everything in the passage combines to drive home this truth to us. As John surveys the scene there is something which immediately focuses his attention. It is the centrality of a throne. But John adds two qualifiers to his description of this throne: it is '*great*' and it is '*white*'.

This is the only time in the whole of the Bible that God's throne is described in this way. It is an imposing and intimidating sight. This is the moment, finally come, when the unrestrained glare and glory of the majesty and holiness of God are revealed in judgement. It is a day of reckoning for sinners.

And John would have us understand that when this moment arrives in the eternal plan of God, it will have un-fathomable consequences for the entire cosmos. Creation itself is undone. The material heavens *('earth and sky')* will flee before the awesome presence of the one who occupies this great white throne. This is the 'uncreation' of the en-tire universe. Time itself will be no more. It is what the apostle Peter describes elsewhere as *'the day of the Lord'*.

> … the day of the Lord will come like a thief. The heavens will disappear with a roar; the elements will be destroyed by fire, and the earth and everything in it will be laid bare.
>
> (2 Pet. 3:10)

There is no escape. There is nowhere to run. There is no place to hide.

It is a matter of paramount importance that we see who appears before this throne.

> 'And I saw the dead, great and small, standing before the throne.'
>
> (Rev. 20:12)

John repeats the phrase *'the dead'* four times in verses 12 and 13. The absence of any qualifying terms here is as striking as their presence when he described the throne in verse 11. The people who stand there are not *'the dead in Christ'* (1 Thess. 4:16), but simply *'the dead'*. The signifi-cance of this will unfold as the judgement proceeds. But notice that the dead are *'**standing**'* before the throne! That is the language of resurrection and this is precisely the scene before us. The situation is one where sinful man is reconstituted to face his maker. Both *'death'* and *'the sea'* relinquish the bodies of those it has claimed. Whether buried in the ground, or a watery grave, it presents no barrier to this summons to judgement. 'Hades' (hell) delivers up the spirits of those it had held captive until the appointed time. This is what Jesus Himself called a rising *'to be condemned'* (John 5:29).

There is no escape and there are no exceptions. *All* the dead, *'great and small'*, stand before the great white throne. Billionaire and beggar appear alongside each other. Whatever distinctions could have been drawn between human beings in the world that has passed, they are of no consequence now.

It is IMPARTIAL

How can we be sure that this judgement will be fair, unbiased and true to the facts? Will judgement and justice go hand in hand?

The answer to these questions is wrapped up in *who* it is that is said to be seated on the great white throne. As you look again at the verses from Revelation 20, it is not difficult to establish the occupant's identity even in the absence of any name or title. This judge sits in a position of absolute power over all creation. He is both separate from creation and sovereign over creation. More than that, this judge has perfect knowledge of all the works of every individual who stands before Him. We can have no hesitation in concluding that this all-powerful and all-knowing judge is God Himself.

But the New Testament has more detail to supply in respect of the divine identity of mankind's judge. Indeed, Jesus Himself has spoken on the matter:

> ... the Father judges no-one, but has entrusted all judgement to the Son, that all may honour the Son just as they

> honour the Father…And he [the Father] has given him
> [the Son] authority to judge because he is the Son of Man.
> (John 5:22-23, 27)

Yes, God is the judge of all mankind but Scripture specifically designates God the Son as the executor of the wrath of God. And the reason why this function resides with *'the Son'* is **because** He is the *'Son of Man'*. On that Day of Judgement, sinners stand before one who is both Son of God and Son of Man. In fact, the term *'Son of Man'* was Jesus' preferred way of referring to Himself when He walked among men.

What is the significance of this?

Firstly, it indicates that the judge had Himself become human. The New Testament is non-negotiable in its teaching that Jesus was fully human, though not merely human. But there is more involved in the title *'Son of Man'* beyond the stressing of Jesus' humanity. *'Son of Man'* was another title for the Messiah who would come. Undoubtedly, the role of the Son of Man/Messiah would be to bring the judgement of God into our world (as described in Daniel chapter 7), but this was not His first function. The Son of Man/Messiah had a rescue mission to accomplish on behalf of sinners before He would sit as their judge. Listen to Jesus:

> … the Son of Man came to seek and to save the lost.
> (Luke 19:10)

> … the Son of Man did not come to be served, but to serve, and to give his life as a ransom for many.
> (Matt. 20:28)

This is who occupies the great white throne on the Day of Judgement! The same one who exchanged the throne of God for the cross of Calvary; the Rescuer who came to experience the wrath of God in the place of sinners; the Saviour who did everything necessary so that sinners might never face punishment for their sins.

But God's just judgement must come. And now this rejected saviour of sinners assumes the role of judge. He who *'knew what was in a man'* (John 2:25) proceeds with absolute integrity and perfect knowledge in His role as the impartial judge.

It is INDIVIDUAL

Our passage in Revelation is emphatic in declaring that *all* sinners will stand before the great white throne and *each* will be judged:

'… The dead were judged according to what they had done …' (20:12)

'… each person was judged according to what he had done.' (20:13)

The unambiguous message of the Bible, from Genesis to Revelation, is that man is accountable to God. We are morally responsible beings. We are answerable for our sin. The universal truth we must come to terms with is that we will all stand before God; one day *I* will stand before God. This is one personal appointment that each of us will be forced to keep:

Man is destined to die once, and after that to face judgement.
(Heb. 9:27)

When talking to someone about Jesus in a one-to-one situation it is not uncommon for other people to 'enter' the conversation. I don't mean that other individuals literally join in the discussion, but they become participants in another sense. Even if the person I am sharing with is personally convinced of who Jesus is and what He has done for them, the conversation can easily switch to the anticipated reaction of family and friends, should they choose to accept Christ as their Lord and Saviour. Another frequent visitor to many a personal conversation is the 'rubbish' Christian. 'I hear what you are saying but I work with someone who says he's a Christian and he ...' 'If you only knew what my auntie did and she sings in the choir!' And so it continues!

I was 18 years old and was just beginning to discover the wonder of what it is to be a child of God. The Bible had come alive to me and I was finding it to be spiritual food for my soul. So, when the day came around for my hospital appointment at the eye clinic, I knew how I would amuse myself in the waiting area. In an effort to be discreet I had brought along my little Gideon Bible. As it happened, my attempt at anonymity was foiled by the large number of people pressed together in the corridor and, in particular, by the rather elderly lady sitting beside me. I was merrily making my way through Paul's letter to the Romans when my reading caught the attention of my fellow-patient. 'Oh it's lovely to see you reading your Bible, son.' My cover was certainly blown, for the unwritten rule appeared to be that nobody spoke to anyone else but just for good measure, the old dear spoke at a volume that people in the car park could have heard! The ensuing conversation was played out in front of everyone else in that corridor. It seemed appropriate to ask my admiring friend, if she was also a Christian. Alas, what followed was a ten-minute (full volume) assassination of her 'Christian' neighbour, who evidently possessed a big Bible and an even bigger mouth!

To this day I am still not sure how much of my response was due to the presence of the Holy Spirit or to the absence of patience! But something had to be said, not only for the benefit of the lady herself, but for all those other observers crammed in the corridor: 'And aren't you so glad you have her as your neighbour! For every time you are faced with Jesus Christ you call to mind your neighbour, with all her failings, and place her between yourself and Christ. That way you don't see Christ and think you don't have to respond to Him.'

Silence. Really awkward silence!

Amazingly, the next words spoken were by the lady herself. 'I suppose you're right, son'. What followed was an impromptu gospel opportunity that I will never forget. Let's all be aware that when the Day of Judgement comes there will be no-one accompanying us. No family, no friend, no enemy. Indeed there will be no neighbour to hide behind. Each and every sinner will stand alone before the judge.

It is INDISPUTABLE

Here in the U.K. hardly a week passes without our hearing the news that some trial has been halted, a case has collapsed, an appeal has been lodged, or compensation has been awarded. There is often more than a little cynicism directed at the effectiveness of the British judicial system by the man on the street. Mention the role of the European Court of Human Rights and you may provoke an expletive or two! However, one thing you can be absolutely sure about is that there will be no challenge brought against the ruling of the court on the Day of Judgement. Justice will be done and will be seen to be done.

If we read carefully the passage in Revelation 20 we see that this is not a trial attempting to get at the truth. *It is a sentencing in full light of the truth.* Not one question is asked. No defence is offered. The sinner is there to hear the declaration of the judge in the face of incontestable evidence brought before the court. There is what we might call both positive and negative evidence convicting the sinner.

The positive evidence comes in the form of what was written in *'the books'*. Clearly these are books of record. They contain God's infallible and complete account of the deeds of every sinner: '… *the dead were judged according to what they had done as recorded in the books'* (v. 12). Each sinner will be confronted by this divine cataloguing of his sins.

But John also sees negative evidence condemning the sinner in the form of what was *not* found written in another book. It is *'the book of life'*. This is a divine record of the redeemed. Jesus told His disciples to rejoice that their names were written in heaven (Luke 10:20). What is written in *'the books'* **accuses** the sinner, but what is not written in *'the book'* **condemns** the sinner:

> Anyone whose name was not found written in the book of life was thrown into the lake of fire.
>
> (Rev. 20:15).

How exceedingly important to grasp this truth: ultimately, sinners are dispatched to the lake of fire, not on account of how enormous nor how numerous their sins, but solely because they had never had their names written in the book of life. They had never come to Christ for salvation. No appeal can be made to the grace of God, for heaven's 'ledger of grace' is empty. It is silent. It has nothing to say on behalf of the condemned.

So many people like to think that there will be some sort of heavenly 'weigh-in' on the Day of Judgement. God will put all the bad stuff on one side of the scales which will, of course, take a dip. But then He will place all the good things we have done on the other side of the scales and (here's hoping!) the scales will tilt in favour of acceptance with God.

Try finding that in the description of the Day of Judgement in Revelation 20!

Seriously, do try to support that version of events against what God has said will happen and you will find it cannot be done. If an individual's name is not written in *'the book of life'* he is destined for the lake of fire. No-one escapes the lake of fire because of what was written in *'the books'*. Acceptance with God has got nothing to do with a sinner accumulating merit with God. Indeed, rather than supporting the sinner's claim to God's approval, the content of *'the books'* is used to determine the extent of the sinner's punishment in the lake of fire. It was Jesus himself who taught that the Day of Judgement will be *'more bearable'* for some sinners than for others. Even the inhabitants of sexually depraved Sodom, destroyed by fire from heaven, will fare better than the privileged people of the village of Capernaum, where Jesus had taught and performed miracles (Matt. 11:20-24). It is worth bearing in mind that God will hold us to account for the 'light' we received and the opportunity we were thus given to accept His offer of salvation in Christ.

It is IRREVOCABLE

Revelation 20 describes the destiny of all whose names were not found written in the book of life as the lake of fire. It then adds: *'The lake of fire is the second death'* (v. 14). The symbolism of *'fire'* is suggestive of the torment inherent in such a destiny. Its description as *'the second death'* drives home the finality of this banishment and separation from God. The full horror of this fate is that it cannot be undone. For all the grotesque inaccuracies of Dante's famous depiction of hell' (Italian, 'inferno') in his 'Divine

Comedy', his inscription over the entrance to the realm of the lost is perfectly correct,

'ABANDON HOPE ALL YE WHO ENTER HERE'

There are some, however, who cling to the 'hope' that the fate of the lost is annihilation. In other words, non-existence will be the eternal penalty of their sins. Complete cessation of being, rather than unending anguish in a lost eternity, is what will follow the Great White Throne judgement. Those who hold such a view believe that the results of this judgement are irrevocable and eternal, but only in the sense that the sinner has become a non-entity. Nothing of the person remains. The sinner is, in the fullest sense of the term 'no more'.

But are they right?

The evidence in the Book of Revelation is far from encouraging. It is an undeniable fact that the apostle John describes five realities as continuing *'forever and ever'*. Each is presented in identical fashion. They are:

- the life of God (4:9; 15:7)

- the reign of Christ (11:15)

- the worship of the saints (1:6; 5:13; 7:12)

- the punishment of Satan (20:10)

- the torment of the lost (14:9-11)

Is it legitimate to give a different meaning to the identical phrase when used in the case of lost sinners? Is that understanding based on what the Bible says, or what we *wish* it said? The truth of the matter is that there is conscious and unending suffering in store for all who are lost.

And the lake of fire has no remedial function. It is retributive in character. It does not make anyone better. No one is reformed by the experience. Sinners do not go there to learn a lesson, but to pay a price. And that price paid is self-aware, eternal and irreversible separation from God.

Thinking things through

It is only when we face the terrible truth of the Day of Judgement that we can begin to appreciate the wonder of the promise that Jesus gave to sinners:

> Very truly I tell you, whoever hears my word and believes him who sent me has eternal life and will not be judged but has crossed over from death to life.
>
> (John 5:24)

To all who repent of their sin, and trust Him for their acceptance with God, Jesus the Judge is even now issuing His *acquittal in advance* of that great Day of Judgement.

QUESTIONS FOR PERSONAL REFLECTION/GROUP DISCUSSION

1. What popular images do people have of the Day of Judgement?

2. Read again the biblical description of the Day of Judgement given in Revelation 20:11-15. What words would you use to describe the scene presented?

3. How can the fact that the Day of Judgement is inescapable both concern and comfort us?

4. Why is Jesus perfectly qualified to sit as judge on the Day of Judgement?

5. What serious point does the story of the old lady and her 'Christian' neighbour make? (p. 100)

6. What role do 'the books' and 'the book of life' play in demonstrating the sinner's guilt on the Day of Judgement? Does the passage offer any hope to those who believe they have lived a 'good' life?

7. Why does the Day of Judgement hold no fear for the Christian? What assurances are given in John 3:16, 5:24 and Romans 8:1?

The Next Step ...

Jesus Christ divides history!

Love and follow Him or loathe and reject Him, we all understand the difference between B.C. and A.D. We talk of that period of world history which was 'Before Christ' against the last two millennia which are measured 'Anno Domini' (in the year of the Lord). But millions of people on our planet insist on going further: not only does Jesus divide human history into two parts but He divides their personal history in the same way. They remember that period of their lives which was 'Before Christ', but they also speak of a new experience – of living life in relationship with Him. It is not just that Christ entered this world some 2,000 years ago and changed history; He has entered *my* world and changed the course of *my* life. Christians can testify that when they received Jesus Christ as Saviour and Lord everything changed. They were brought into the experience the apostle Paul describes in 2 Corinthians 5:17:

> … if anyone is in Christ, the new creation has come: the old has gone, the new is here!

By this stage you will have considered some of the most fundamental reasons why it makes sense for you to make that same commitment to Jesus Christ. Perhaps it is the case that you are convinced that such a decision makes sense and now is the time to respond to Jesus. How do you go about doing that? How do you become a Christian?

Once again, we must allow the Bible to guide us in this all-important matter. In Acts 20:21 Paul summed up his years of service for God in this way:

> I have declared to both Jews and Greeks that they must turn to God in repentance and have faith in our Lord Jesus.

All that God asks of us is that we come to Him willing to turn from our sin and trusting in Jesus to save us. God offers His *'great salvation'* (Heb. 2:3) to those who face the seriousness of their sin; who appreciate that their lives have fallen short of His standard and offended His holiness and who are willing to accept their guilt but desire to be forgiven, cleansed and set free. So as we come to God burdened by our sin, we are convinced that Jesus is the answer! Our entire hope rests upon Jesus the Son of God who died and rose again to secure our salvation. We take God at His word: if we believe in the Lord Jesus we will be saved (John 3:16; Acts 16:30-31; Rom. 10:9).

A word of caution ...

Jesus himself bids us *'count the cost'* involved in coming to Him (Luke 14:25-33). It means the end of self-rule, for we take up our cross and follow Him. Jesus will freely grant us what this world can never give; lasting peace, true joy, certain hope and eternal life. But make no mistake, our world can take away many 'passing' things: popularity, status, wealth, prospects. For many people choosing Christ can turn this world into a hard place. If you want proof of that you should check out an organisation such as Open Doors which exists to support persecuted Christians worldwide (www.opendoorsuk.org). To come to Christ is never an easy decision. It is, however, always the right one.

Further help:

Read the Bible – The Bible itself states that its purpose is to make us *'wise for salvation through faith in Christ Jesus'* (2 Tim. 3:15). As a starting point, why not commit to reading one of the four Gospels and acquainting yourself more closely with what Jesus did and said? So much more could have been written about Jesus in this book! For instance, we have not even touched upon the role of the Son of God in the creation of the universe or His present ministry in heaven for His people and little has been said about his inevitable return to our world. The Bible is the source of all this information and truth. Read it!

Seek out Christians – Don't be afraid to approach someone you know to be a Christian, perhaps the person who gave you this book, and tell them you are thinking about the claims of Jesus. Locate a Bible-teaching church that is active in sharing the good news of Jesus. Many churches run courses such as 'Christianity Explored' (www.christianityexplored.org) which will bring you into contact with Christians (and other individuals who want to find out more).

Get in touch – please feel free to address any enquiries to: whyjesus.geoffmcilrath@gmail.com

And finally …

Be honest with yourself! Nothing is more important than your response to Jesus Christ. No issue is more pressing. No decision has greater consequences. Don't make excuses and don't put it off. *Examine the evidence and follow where it leads you.*

Glossary

Atheism – the belief in the non-existence of God or gods

Calvary – the place where Jesus was crucified (outside the city of Jerusalem)

Child of God – someone who has been born (again) into the family of God through faith in Christ

Faith – trust, reliance, dependence

Grace – undeserved kindness

Just – in accordance with the requirements of justice, perfectly righteous

Justified – to be declared right with God

Materialism – the belief that all of reality can be explained by material processes

Messiah – Anointed One, God's promised rescuer

New Testament – the words of God written down after the coming of Christ

Old Testament – the words of God written down before the coming of Christ

Rationalism – a reliance on human reason and rejection of divine revelation

Repentance – a complete change of mind, a turning from sin to God

Righteousness – free from moral imperfection, holy, in right relation to God

Salvation – a comprehensive term to describe God's rescue of sinners

Sanhedrin – Jewish supreme council and ultimate authority in religious matters

Saviour – rescuer, deliverer

Sin – our disobedience and state of rebellion against God

The gospel – the good news about Jesus the Saviour

The redeemed – all those purchased by God through the blood of Christ

Further Reading

Craig L. Blomberg, *The Historical Reliability of the Gospels*, IVP Academic, 2007

John C. Lennox, *Gunning for God*, Lion, 2011

C. S. Lewis, *Mere Christianity*, William Collins, 2012

Josh McDowell, *Evidence for Christianity*, Thomas Nelson, 2006

David Robertson, *Magnificent Obsession*, Christian Focus, 2013

John R. W. Stott, *The Cross of Christ*, IVP, 2006

John R. W. Stott, *Why I am a Christian*, IVP, 2003

Christian Focus Publications

Our mission statement –

STAYING FAITHFUL
In dependence upon God we seek to impact the world through literature faithful to His infallible Word, the Bible. Our aim is to ensure that the Lord Jesus Christ is presented as the only hope to obtain forgiveness of sin, live a useful life and look forward to heaven with Him.

Our books are published in four imprints:

CHRISTIAN
FOCUS

Popular works including biographies, commentaries, basic doctrine and Christian living.

CHRISTIAN
HERITAGE

Books representing some of the best material from the rich heritage of the church.

MENTOR

Books written at a level suitable for Bible College and seminary students, pastors, and other serious readers. The imprint includes commentaries, doctrinal studies, examination of current issues and church history.

CF4•K

Children's books for quality Bible teaching and for all age groups: Sunday school curriculum, puzzle and activity books; personal and family devotional titles, biographies and inspirational stories – because you are never too young to know Jesus!

Christian Focus Publications Ltd,
Geanies House, Fearn, Ross-shire,
IV20 1TW, Scotland, United Kingdom.
www.christianfocus.com
blog.christianfocus.com